LIFE IN SPACE?

DISASTER FROM THE SKIES?

Join the phenomenal Ripley team as they explore the almost unbelievable and often unexplained secrets of our planet, our solar system, and the infinite reaches of outer space.

Ripley's Believe It or Not! titles

Ripley's Believe It or Not! 28th Series
Ripley's Believe It or Not! 29th Series
Ripley's Believe It or Not! 30th Series
Ripley's Believe It or Not! Ghosts, Witches and ESP
Ripley's Believe It or Not! Great Disasters
Ripley's Believe It or Not! Stars, Space and UFOs

Published by POCKET BOOKS

RIPLEY's
Believe It or Not!®

STARS SPACE UFOs

PUBLISHED BY POCKET BOOKS NEW YORK

Another *Original* publication of POCKET BOOKS

POCKET BOOKS, a Simon & Schuster division of
GULF & WESTERN CORPORATION
1230 Avenue of the Americas, New York, N.Y. 10020

ISBN: 0-671-46219-9

First Pocket Books printing September, 1978

10 9 8 7 6 5

POCKET and colophon are registered trademarks
of Simon & Schuster.

Interior design by Sofia Grunfeld

Printed in the U.S.A.

Contents

Introduction   11

The Universe   21

The Galaxy   35

The Super Stars   45

The Stars   51

The Sun   81

The Planets   93

The Earth   113

The Moon   139

Spaceships   153

Glossary   187

"Look at the stars! Look, look up at the skies!
O, look at all the fire-folk sitting in the air!"

—Gerard Manley Hopkins
(1844–1889)

STARS
SPACE
UFOs

Introduction

Did you ever look up at the sky—and wonder what's really out there?

Have you seen films of the astronauts—and wondered how it feels to be weightless? And how exciting it must be to explore other worlds in space?

Have you heard about UFO sightings—and wondered if we are being contacted by beings from millions of miles away?

Right now mankind is just beginning to explore outer space. We have the tools and the intelligence. We have already set foot on the moon. Our space ships have landed on Mars. Soon we will visit Venus and the other planets. Before long the entire solar system might be "home" to us earthlings. And then—certainly within the next 50 years —we will be ready to reach out . . . into deepest space. What will we find? Is there life out there? Whom will we encounter? What amazing adventures await us?

This book is an attempt to answer these questions—and to prepare you for the greatest adventure of all time . . . the exploration of space.

Galileo

UNRAVELING THE SECRETS

The mysteries of space that puzzled the early Greeks and Egyptians were often explained mathematically. Some of their calculations were quite accurate. For instance, the ancient Egyptians knew the year was 365¼ days long; in 134 B.C. the Greek astronomer Hipparchus correctly calculated the distance to the moon; the Greeks even believed the Earth was round (by watching the Earth's shadow cross the moon during an eclipse), and they believed it *1900 years before Columbus!*

Yet some of their misconceptions continued to be believed for centuries. Even as late as the 16th century Copernicus' theory that the Earth revolves around the sun was thought to be heresy! But with the invention of the telescope in the early 17th century an era of truly scientific study of the Heavens began.

In 1609, Galileo was the first man to see the craters of the moon, the Giant Red Spot, and the four moons of Jupiter.

In 1655 the rings of Saturn were discovered by Christian Huyghens.

And by 1685 Sir Isaac Newton had devised the theory of Universal Gravity, the first understanding of one of the most essential forces in the Universe.

Now, 300 years later, a new era is beginning. For the first time we have studied the actual substance of the moon and of Mars. We have measured and observed more than half of the planets

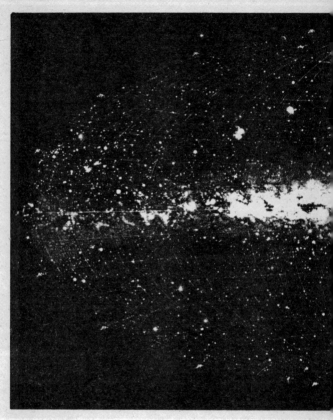

Looking for the North Pole? *You can find it in the sky!*
The star map that scientists use has both a *north*
galactic pole and a *south* galactic pole!

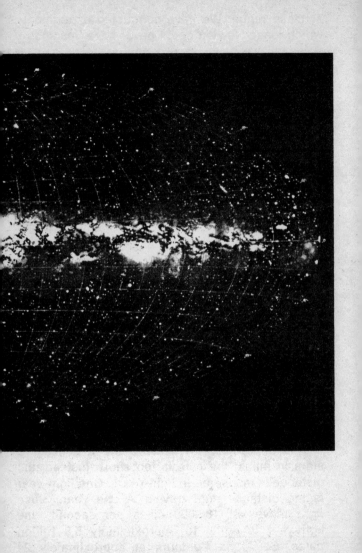

at close range. We have conducted experiments which Isaac Newton could never have imagined.

But all we have learned only leads us to new mysteries, more puzzling than all the questions which have been answered!

UNIMAGINABLE DISTANCE!

Understanding the size of the solar system isn't easy. If the sun were the size of an apple, the Earth would be over 30 feet away and no larger than a grain of sand. Jupiter would be the size of a cherry pit 200 feet from the apple. And little Pluto would be a speck of dust circling the apple at a distance of a half mile!

If this is the size of the solar system, how far away are the stars? Alpha Centauri, our closest stellar neighbor, is approximately 24 trillion miles away! In relation to our apple-centered solar system, Alpha Centauri would be the size of another apple, but over 1,000 miles distant! Of all the stars in the sky, only 50 stars are closer than 100 trillion miles! All others are still farther away . . . much farther!

It is impossible to measure the distances to stars in miles; the mile is too short. Instead, the distance is measured in light-years. One light-year is the distance light travels in one year. Since light moves at 186,000 miles per second, one light-year is equal to approximately 5.8 trillion miles. So Alpha Centauri, at approximately 24 trillion miles distance, is about 4.3 light-years away.

FAMOUS WOODCUT
MADE IN NUREMBERG,
GERMANY OVER
<u>400 YEARS AGO</u>

SHOWS NEARLY A DOZEN
UFOS IN THE SKY!

PRESIDENT JIMMY CARTER HAD A PERSONAL *UFO* SIGHTING OCT. 1969! HE DESCRIBED A BRIGHT OBJECT ABOUT THE SIZE OF THE MOON. "IF I BECOME PRESIDENT," HE PROMISED, "I'LL MAKE EVERY PIECE OF INFORMATION THIS COUNTRY HAS ABOUT *UFOs* AVAILABLE TO THE PUBLIC AND SCIENTISTS."

Some people can't believe the enormous size of the Universe, even when presented with the facts. Others find it difficult to believe in the phenomena we call Unidentified Flying Objects, or UFOs. In this book we are presenting the mysteries of unexplained events and UFO sightings side by side with the mysteries of space.

And who is to say *what* is incredible?

Here is the evidence.

Believe It or Not!

The
Universe

IS THE UNIVERSE A BOX OR A NUT . . . ?

Had you asked the ancient Egyptians what the Universe was like you might have received two answers. Most of them believed it was a large rectangular box supported on strong pillars. Those who lived in part of the Nile Delta, however, thought the Universe was the body of a goddess named Nut.

. . . OR IS IT A ZOO?

The ancient Hindus, however, thought of the Universe differently. They believed it to be an ocean with a floating serpent . . . on whose back was a turtle's shell . . . on which stood four elephants . . . who carried the Earth on their backs! Nobody speculated what might have happened had the serpent rolled over . . .

HOW DID WE GET HERE?

How was the solar system formed? One of the earliest theories, made by the 18th century French mathematician LaPlace, was that the sun threw off material as it rotated. According to LaPlace, this process was repeated several times and the material eventually condensed into our planets. A second theory, developed early in this century, is that another star once passed by our sun, drawing out some of the sun's material which later became the planets. This theory states that the material was cigar-shaped and that when it cooled the larger parts of it were in the middle— an idea that may account for the larger sizes of Jupiter and Saturn! Still another theory states that the sun drew material out of another star and forced this material to revolve around it. Again, the material condensed and became our planets.

. . . The age of the Universe is nearly 20 billion years—that's how long ago it exploded. Life on Earth has only existed for about four billion years. That means there may be other worlds besides ours—and, if they're older, they would have more time to evolve higher forms of life! . . .

THE SOVIET UNION COMPLETED CONSTRUCTION ON
**THE WORLD'S LARGEST REFRACTING
TELESCOPE** IN 1970. THE COLOSSAL INSTRUMENT
IS **80 FEET LONG**
AND WEIGHS **935 TONS!**
THROUGH ITS 236.2-INCH LENS YOU CAN SEE
THE FLICKERING OF A CANDLE
AT A DISTANCE OF 15,000 MILES.

THOUSANDS OF PEOPLE SAW UFOs OBSERVING THE ATOMIC PROVING GROUNDS AT LOS ALAMOS, NEW MEXICO! RECENTLY DECLASSIFIED AIR FORCE DOCUMENTS REVEALED AN *AMAZING NUMBER* OF UFO OBSERVATIONS DURING 1948-49... *BUT THEY NEVER INTERFERED!*

IS SPACE REALLY EMPTY?

Is the space between celestial bodies filled with matter of some sort or is it merely a vacuum? From what scientists have come up with so far, interstellar space may be filled with as much as 10% of the entire matter of the Universe, and this matter is estimated to be 1% dust and 99% gas.

THE EXPANDING UNIVERSE

The first person to measure the enormous scale of the Universe was astronomer Edwin Hubble, in 1923. He found that by comparing the brightness of stars, he could compute their distance. According to Hubble's discoveries, our cosmos is vanishing outward into space like a puff of smoke!

THE CASE OF THE RACING NEBULAE

In 1930 Hubble discovered some nebulae—celestial bodies of gas and dust—that were rushing away from Earth at the speed of two or three thousand miles per second. In March of 1931, someone else claimed he had seen an 8,000-miles-per-second nebula. In December of that same

EARTH'S BEST OBSERVATORY
Looking for a good place to watch the stars? Why not try *Kitt Peak National Observatory in Arizona.* The observatory has several telescopes—including one with a scope of four meters (or almost *five yards!*)

year Dr. Milton Humason of Mount Wilson Observatory won the race with his report of having seen two nebulae speeding away from Earth at the rate of 15,000 miles per second!

BRINGING THE UNIVERSE
DOWN TO EARTH

Who invented the telescope? Most people think it was Jan Lippershey, a 17th-century Dutch lens-grinder. Others think it may have been Roger Bacon who invented it as early as 1260! However, no one has been able to prove who the real inventor was—and the origin of the telescope is still a mystery!

The famed astronomer Galileo did not invent the telescope, but he created over 100 of them, and his work revolutionized the entire field of astronomy. Believe it or not, the telescope Galileo himself used was less powerful than today's average binoculars!

Ever wonder why telescopes are located at high altitudes? Because of problems caused by the Earth's atmosphere. Clouds and other air masses obstruct vision and distort images in the sky. A group of Princeton astrophysicists, headed by Martin Schwartzchild, once traveled up in a balloon to get clearer photographs of the sun, aware of the problems of photographing from the surface of the Earth. They took a 12-inch telescope and flew at a height of 80,000 feet! Ground-based optical telescopes would have revealed indistinct

ACCORDING TO THE
GALLUP POLL...
OVER 5,000,000 AMERICANS
CLAIM TO HAVE ACTUALLY
SEEN A UFO. AND NEARLY
HALF OF THE POPULATION
BELIEVES IN THEIR EXISTENCE!

images due to time variations in the refraction of a light ray passing through the Earth's atmosphere. At 80,000 feet, this problem was minimized.

WHEN DID WE FIRST GET A PHOTO OF OUTER SPACE?

The first photo of the moon was taken at Harvard Observatory in 1841. But it was not until photography was applied to other stars and planets that its real benefits were known. The camera is able to record lights invisible to the human eye—and can also display simultaneously all the objects it photographs.

LIGHTS . . . CAMERA . . . STARS!

Contrary to popular belief, the advantage of a larger telescope is not greater magnification. Instead, it is the telescope's larger lens, which gathers more light.

The world's largest reflecting telescope, at Mount Palomar, California, is used to capture the light from distant galaxies. The instrument is one of man's miracles of construction. Its concave lens mirror is nearly 17 feet across and is shaped to an accuracy of a millionth of an inch! It weighs 500 tons, or 1,000,000 pounds, yet it is so delicately mounted that an electric motor of just a few inches in size can move it!

U.S. DEPT. OF DEFENSE

THE DEFENSE DEPARTMENT STILL
KEEPS TABS ON UFO SIGHTINGS...
EVEN IN IRAN! ON SEPT. 19, 1976
AT LEAST FIVE PEOPLE SAW A UFO
OVER THE SKIES OF TEHRAN, IRAN.
BUT THE INFORMATION WAS KEPT
TOP SECRET FOR ALMOST A YEAR
AFTER THE INCIDENT!

England's giant dish antenna at Jodrell Bank is the world's largest steerable radio telescope. The dish antenna enables astronomers to track orbiting astronauts and to detect objects billions of light-years away!

SECRET CODES . . . FROM OUTER SPACE!

Giant radio telescopes all over the world have picked up what seem to be coded messages from deep in outer space. Soviet astronomer Nikolai S. Kardashev says the signals originate from two celestial objects called CTA-21 and CTA-102. Kardashev is on record as saying, "The signals could only be communications from intelligent beings."

The
Galaxy

THE MILKY WAY

The Milky Way is not just a chocolate-covered candy bar! It is also the name of our galaxy. Harlow Shapely was the first to chart this galaxy and the task took him three years, from 1914 to 1917.

The stars in the Milky Way are revolving constantly around a center which is approximately 28,000 light-years away from the sun. The width of the Milky Way is about 100,000 light-years, or nearly 580,000,000,000,000,000 miles!

Our galaxy is believed to contain 150 billion stars—which represents only a small part of the Universe! Scientists estimate there are at least *100 billion galaxies,* some as far as 6 billion light-years away.

AT LEAST **62** AMERICAN ASTRONOMY PROFESSORS REVEAL THAT THEY HAVE ACTUALLY SIGHTED AND RECORDED UFOs! ONE SCIENTIST REPORTED SIGHTING A "FLAT, SILVER GRAY" UFO WHILE DRIVING IN NEW MEXICO. WHEN HE TRIED TO GET CLOSE TO THE OBJECT, HIS CAR'S ENGINE SUDDENLY QUIT..._SOMETHING IT HAD NEVER DONE BEFORE_!

THE YOUTH OF OUR GALAXY . . .

The youngest stars in our galaxy are the Pleiades cluster of stars. They were born only 60 million years ago . . . just about the time when man's ancestors were taking to the trees!

HOW FAR CAN YOU SEE?

Most of the individual stars of the Milky Way are too faint to be seen by the naked eye, but together they make a faintly lit belt about the sky. The Andromeda Galaxy is much further away than the Milky Way. Its individual stars are only barely visible through a telescope. But *en masse,* the Andromeda Galaxy can be seen by the naked eye. Thus, if anyone asks you how far you can see, give them an answer of around 2,000,000 light-years!

SINCE 1947, UFO EXPERTS HAVE
REPORTED A *CYCLE OF SIGHTINGS*
...*EVERY 64 MONTHS!* 1947, 1953,
1958, 1964, 1968, 1973 A<u>ND</u> 1978!

OUR SUN IS *SO DISTANT* FROM THE CENTER
OF THE MILKY WAY THAT LIGHT TAKES
30,000 YEARS TO REACH US FROM THERE.

THE JET IN THE SKY!

Scientists have discovered a brilliant jet of light extending from the nucleus of the far distant galaxy Virgo-A. This jet expends an enormous amount of energy and is equivalent to the radiation emitted from millions and millions of stars. In order to power this jet, an equivalent of approximately *100 suns* would have to be drained!

The sun is only one star in the Milky Way, a galaxy or grouping of over 100 billion stars. The sun, like each of these stars, revolves around the center point of the Milky Way, much like the planets revolve around the sun. But even though our sun is circling at 200 miles per second, it takes 200 million years for the sun to make one full trip!

On a clear night you can see the Milky Way as a white band arching across the sky. It appears to us to be a band because we are inside it. If you were inside a dinner plate somewhere near the rim, and tried to see to the far rim of the plate, you would be looking through the entire plate. If you looked out toward the top or the bottom of the plate, there would be much less to be looking through. Thus, when looking at the Milky Way, you are looking at the far side of our galaxy.

As dinner plates go, the Milky Way would make a big one. It's over 100,000 light-years across—the same distance, written in miles, is 580,000,-000,000,000,000 miles!

NEW YORK'S BIG BLACKOUT OF 1977 WAS CAUSED BY UFOs ... ACCORDING TO SEVERAL OBSERVERS. TEN MINUTES BEFORE THE BLACKOUT, STRANGE UFOS WERE SIGHTED NEAR THE WORLD TRADE CENTER ... IN MINUTES THE CITY WAS IN TOTAL DARKNESS!

But even 100,000 light-years is a short distance compared with the distance to the nearest other galaxy or star cluster. The Andromeda Galaxy, the galaxy nearest to the Milky Way, is over two *million* light-years away!

Though Andromeda is the only other galaxy that can be seen with the naked eye, others can be seen through telescopes. Twenty galaxies, with hundreds of billions of stars each, are grouped within our immediate neighborhood— meaning closer than 3 million light-years! The next nearest group of galaxies is a cluster of 2,500 galaxies, 60 million light-years away! Three hundred million light-years away is a cluster of 10,000 galaxies with between ten billion and 100 billion stars in each galaxy!

How many of these stars have planets? How many of those planets sustain life? The Universe is so vast—and the mysteries of space so many— that we seem to create new questions faster than we can answer the old ones. We may never have all the answers.

The
Super
Stars

1054—
the Crab Nebula was observed in China and Japan when people saw a blinding flash of light in the sky.

1572—
Tycho saw a star exploding and named it after himself.

1604—
Kepler noticed a nova and also named it for himself.

What do these three stars have in common?
Why are they so unusual?

Each of these stars became a supernova—a star that usually begins small, blue, and fainter but hotter than the sun, and suddenly becomes ten or even several hundred million times brighter before it gradually fades away. The three mentioned above all occurred in our own galaxy—and the last two were only 32 years apart!

THE **THIRD BRIGHTEST OBJECT EVER TO APPEAR IN THE HEAVENS...** _THE GREAT NOVA OF JULY 4,1054 A.D._ THIS GIANT EXPLODING STAR APPEARED _SIX TIMES BRIGHTER_ THAN THE PLANET VENUS AND WAS ONLY OUTSHONE BY THE SUN AND MOON. FOR 23 DAYS THE GREAT NOVA COULD BE OBSERVED IN _BROAD DAYLIGHT!_

WHAT HAPPENS WHEN A STAR EXPLODES?

In the year 1054 A.D. a star exploded. Today, over *900 years later*, we can *still see* the results of that explosion! It's called the Crab Nebula—and it's one of the most interesting sights in the sky.

When a supernova explodes it releases energy at almost 10,000,000,000 times the rate of the sun. If an object happened to be five light-years away from the exploding star, it would pick up a tenth as much energy as the Earth receives from the sun—and would have an especially hot year! The heat of an exploding supernova is so great that it converts base metals (such as iron) to precious metals (such as gold)!

ONE MILLION SUPER STARS!

In an average galaxy it is estimated that there are approximately three supernovas per century. Thus, in 33 million years an average galaxy will have about one million supernovas!

The
Stars

STAR SPEED

The stars in our Universe are constantly in motion and move at an astonishing rate. Why then do they appear to be standing still? The reason is simple—they're so extremely far away. It would take hundreds of thousand of years for us to detect a particular star's movement!

STAR LIGHT—STAR BRIGHT!

What is the brightest star? Of approximately 7,000 stars visible to the naked eye on Earth, Sirius is brightest. However, in terms of true brilliance, Deneb—in the constellation Cygnus—is the most brilliant star we know.

The brilliance (or watt power) of the stars varies widely, from the astronomical equivalent of a glow-worm to a powerful searchlight. Using this scale, our sun is only slightly less than medium bright—or about the intensity of a night-light!

In fact, our sun is one of the least bright stars in the stellar system. If it were just a little closer, the star Alpha Centauri would give you a tan in just a few minutes.

AUTHORITIES NOW BELIEVE THAT UFOs HAVE LANDED ON EARTH AND ALIENS ARE LIVING AMONG US!

AFTER 15 YEARS OF STUDY, SPACE EXPERT TIMOTHY GREEN BECKLEY SAYS UFOs MAKE CONTACT WITH HUMANS.

IN OCTOBER, 1956, HARRY STURDEVANT, A NIGHT
WATCHMAN AT A TRENTON, N.J. CONSTRUCTION
FIRM, BECAME *THE FIRST PERSON TO
RECEIVE WORKMAN'S COMPENSATION AS
A RESULT OF HAVING BEEN "ASSAULTED BY
A UFO"!* ON THE EVENING OF OCTOBER 2,
STURDEVANT SPIED A DISTANT RED LIGHT IN
THE SKY HURTLING TOWARD HIM. STURDEVANT
WAS OVERCOME BY A VILE ODOR AND COLLAP-
SED WITH ACUTE STOMACH PAINS. A NEW
JERSEY WORKMAN'S COMPENSATION REFEREE
RULED THAT THIS EXTRAORDINARY CLAIM WAS
LEGITIMATE AND *TRUE!*

"3C273 . . . 3C273 . . . BURNING BRIGHT!"

In 1963, researchers discovered a star that is a million-million times brighter than the sun. It does not affect us as the sun does, however, because it is about 1.5 billion light-years away. Scientists have given this star a number name—3C273.

Light travels at the speed of 186,000 miles per second. If the star you are looking at is 650 light-years away, that means that it takes 650 years for the light emitted by that star to reach the Earth and come into your window.

STARS: HOT AND NOT-SO-HOT

Why do some stars look red and some white? Because the bigger "red giants" have large surfaces on which to distribute the energy they produce; they have lower temperatures and a red color. On the other hand, the smaller "white dwarfs" are so hot they glow with a brilliant white light.

What are white dwarfs? No, not Snow White's little friends, but shrunken stars. One such dwarf, the "companion of Sirius," has a globe of about the same size as the Earth's. This globe, however, contains a mass equivalent to that of our sun. Given this extraordinary concentration of matter, a thimbleful of matter from Sirius' companion

IF YOU COULD COLLECT **ALL THE STARS** IN THE UNIVERSE IN ONE SPOT, THE SCALE WOULD READ 100,000,000,000,000,000,000,000,000,000,000,000,000,000,000,000,000 *TONS!*

would weigh in excess of one hundred pounds on Earth!

There is no way to determine the exact density of a single star. Only in a two-star system can the mass be found. How? By following the orbital paths of the two stars.

CELESTIAL TWINS!

Double stars are like twins, even though separated by vast distances in space. Some scientists believe that the resemblance of two stars to each

other can be so great that communication between the two stars—like telepathic contact between two people—could exist.

HOW MANY STARS CAN YOU NAME?

Every star has a name. In 1918 the Henry Draper
Catalogue published a list of 225,000 stars, their
names and their position in the heavens!

WHAT ARE THE ODDS?

Every star possesses a system of planets. There
must, therefore, be millions of planets in our own
galaxy and there are an infinite number of galaxies. It is highly probable that some of these
planets have physical conditions almost identical
with those on our Earth.

THE STARS—NEAR AND FAR

When you look out of your window on a clear,
moonless night, the stars you are seeing could
be anywhere from 4.3 light-years away to 8 billion
light-years away. Alpha Centauri, a triple-star system, is the nearest and scientists at one time believed that the most distant stars we could see
were 5 billion light-years from Earth . . . meaning
the light from the furthest stars, traveling at more
than *670 million miles per hour,* would require
5 billion years to reach our telescopes! Now new,

more powerful celestial bodies have been discovered. Called quasars, they are more than 8 billion light-years away. Quasars resemble stars, but emit unusually bright blue and ultraviolet light, as well as radio waves. To reach our telescopes the light from a quasar would have to have started toward us billions of years ago—even before Earth was created.

Stars vary not only in their distance and luminosity but also in their size. Van Maaren's star, 13 light-years away, is smaller than the Earth (its diameter is 75% that of the Earth) and it is about 10,000 times fainter than the sun.

ARE YOU LOOKING AT A DEAD STAR?

The stars you see in the sky may no longer exist! A star that is, say, 400 light-years away from the Earth may have died 300 years ago. Since it takes 400 years for the light to get here, the star will remain visible to us on Earth for another 100 years!

GUESS WHO'S COMING TO DINNER!

Scientists have suggested that since there may be several billion planets in our galaxy alone, there is an overwhelming probability that we are being visited by beings from elsewhere in our solar system.

In 1820 Karl Friedrich Gauss (1777-1855), one of history's greatest mathematicians, proposed that hundreds of square miles in the Siberian steppes be planted with long lines of pine trees symbolically illustrating the Pythagorean theorem. The distinctive pattern, Gauss reasoned, would make it clear to observers on other planets that the earth is inhabited by intelligent life.

Professor Weizsacker, a famous German astronomer, declared in 1943 that it was be strange if life did *not* exist on other planets in our galaxy.

Billy Graham, the famous evangelist, firmly believes that intelligent life is thriving on other planets. He says we have nothing to fear from them. They are constantly depicted in science fiction as bizarre creatures, but he feels it more likely that they are more advanced than we and would come in peace. They might even bring solutions to the problems we face on Earth: disease, war and environmental pollution. Dr. Graham bases his startling conclusions not only on his own deep religious beliefs, but also on discussions with leading U.S. space experts!

THE CANDIDATE FROM OUTER SPACE!

In 1960 Gabriel Green decided to become a presidential candidate because he was asked, he claims, by a representative from one of the planets of Alpha Centauri. Green reported that he was sitting in his home in California when someone knocked at the door and introduced himself as being a visitor from Alpha Centauri. When asked if he would run for office, Gabe unhesitatingly answered "yes." Needless to say, this decision prompted numerous phone calls from Alpha Centauri concerning campaign strategy! As to why he was chosen, Gabe had no answer but perhaps being president of the Amalgamated Flying Saucers Club of America didn't hurt . . . One final note: according to Gabe, "Earth women just don't compare to Alpha Centauri females."

Well, you're familiar with the term light-headed and by now you know about light-years—how about light-feet? Every light-foot is the distance light travels in one *billionth* of a second!

CREATURE FROM OUTER SPACE IS CAPTURED!

THE U.S. GOVERNMENT CAPTURED A CRASHED UFO IN 1948 AND _FOUND A DEAD SPACE BEING INSIDE_. THE CREATURE WAS DESCRIBED AS SMALL—ABOUT 4 FT. 6-INCHES, HAIRLESS AND HAD NO THUMBS. THE AIR FORCE SUBMITTED A FULL REPORT TO THE CIA, _BUT HID IT FROM THE AMERICAN PUBLIC!_

THE FIRST FLYING SAUCERS

The term "flying saucer" was used as early as January 24, 1878, by John Martin, a Texas farmer residing near Denison, Texas. Mr. Martin happened to have observed a dark flying object shaped like a disc traveling at a high speed in the sky. He used the word "saucer" to describe it.

ON NOV. 11, 1975, *FOR THE FIRST TIME EVER*, JOINT AMERICAN AND CANADIAN FORCES USED RADAR TO *TRACK A UFO!* THE UFO, WHICH WAS SPOTTED IN ONTARIO, CANADA, REMAINED ON THE RADAR SCREENS *FOR 6 HOURS!*

In 1896 and 1897 the United States was inundated with eyewitness reports of mysterious airships flying over cities and farms. These sightings are often explained by the fact that many Americans were eagerly anticipating the first successful flights of lighter-than-air crafts. Nonetheless, it was reported that some of these ships landed or were found on the ground with their inhabitants, all of whom appeared to be *normal human beings!* The descriptions of the objects supposedly seen corresponded closely to cigar-shaped dirigibles that many people thought the first aircraft would look like. Although most newspapers of the time considered the airship sightings the result of fevered imaginations, these sightings were never adequately explained. Today most experts are considering them the first reported mass sightings of UFOs in the United States.

UFOs THE WORLD OVER

Since May, 1946 every country in the world has reported UFO sightings. No explanation has, however, been found for these strange objects and people.

There are 100 world-wide UFO sightings every day according to Ted Phillips of the Center for UFO studies of Northwestern University. And at least twice that number are never reported!

In a recent Stanford University survey, led by Dr. Peter A Sturrock, an astrophysicist, 80% of the 1,356 scientists questioned declared that the UFO phenomenon is based on fact. And 62 of the

A BULLET *TURNED INSIDE OUT* CONVINCES
POLICE THAT A UFO FRIGHTENED CARL HIGDON
ALMOST TO DEATH! THE 41-YEAR-OLD MAN
INSISTS *HE WAS ABDUCTED BY ALIEN BEINGS
AND WHISKED TO ANOTHER PLANET!* HE WAS
HUNTING FOR ELK IN WYOMING WHEN THEY
LANDED, BUT THE BULLET HE SHOT AT AN ELK
STARTED TO "*FLOAT*" OUT OF THE BARREL.
BALLISTIC EXPERTS COULD FIND NO OTHER
EXPLANATION FOR THE CONDITION OF THE
SHELL THAT HAD BEEN *TURNED INSIDE OUT!*

scientists actually reported their own sightings of strange objects in space!

One professor confessed that he, his brother, an uncle and six policemen chased a UFO for over an hour in Ontario, Canada. They arrived at a large tree and noticed that the object appeared to be examining the tree. The astronomer said that the object seemed "to be governed by some intelligence."

The Stanford University study also includes a description of a "flat, silver gray" UFO that was sighted by a scientist driving in New Mexico. When he attempted to get close to the object, his car's engine suddenly quit—something it had never done before!

80% of U.S. astronomers believe UFO's exist and should be investigated.

A PROFESSOR OF ASTRONOMY AT NORTHWESTERN
UNIVERSITY CLAIMS THAT _AIR FORCE OFFICIALS
REFUSE TO ACCEPT REPORTS OF UFO CREATURES!_
PROF. J. ALLEN HYNEK, TECHNICAL ADVISOR FOR
THE FILM "CLOSE ENCOUNTERS" AND OFFICIAL
CONSULTANT TO THE AIR FORCE, THINKS THAT
THE AIR FORCE SIMPLY _DOESN'T WANT TO
DEAL WITH THE POSSIBILITY OF BEINGS FROM
OUTER SPACE!_

ITEM:

April 20, 1897, LeRoy, Kansas: Alexander Hamilton, his son, Wall, and his tenant, Gid Heslip, were awakened by a noise among the cattle. Looking out the window they saw a cigar-shaped airship descending upon the cow herd. The three ran outside toward the corral armed with axes. Meanwhile, the airship was 30 feet above the herd. The three could see six strange-looking beings talking but could not understand what they were saying. Upon seeing the three men, the vessel rose to 300 feet and hovered over a two-year-old heifer which had apparently become stuck in the wire fence. When the men reached the heifer they found a cable about a half inch thick (made of some red material) around her neck—with the other end leading to the vessel. The men tried to slip the noose loose but couldn't; instead, they untangled the wire from the heifer. Once freed, the spaceship and heifer rose slowly and disappeared over a hill. A day later, while Mr. Hamilton was out looking for his heifer, a neighbor informed him he had found the heifer's hide, legs, and head in a nearby field.

FOUR WITNESSES REPORTED A
UFO LANDING IN DELPHOS, KANSAS
IN 1977!
AFTER THE SIGHTING, NOTHING COULD
GROW IN THE SOIL...THE CALCIUM
CONTENT WAS *10 TIMES* MORE THAN
NORMAL!

ITEM:

February 9, 1913. Canada: A most extraordinary procession passed through the skies of Canada and elsewhere during this night. According to a Professor Chant of the Royal Astronomical Society, a group of unknown objects carrying lights was seen from Saskatchewan to the island of Bermuda. The procession was described "like an old express train, lighted at night. The lights were at different points, one in front, a rear light, then a succession of lights in the tail." These objects gave off sounds that were heard on the ground. This lasted from three to five minutes over the sky of Toronto. A long-time observer of meteors, W. F. Denning, wrote in the *Journal of the RAS of Canada* that, at that time, he had never seen meteors of such a type in over 40 years of study. They moved at a velocity that cannot be compared with that of meteors.

<u>SEVEN MEN</u>, OUT FOR A NIGHT WALK IN
THE ITALIAN COUNTRYSIDE IN AUGUST, 1977,
CLAIM TO HAVE BEEN CONFRONTED BY A
HUMANOID ALMOST EIGHT FEET TALL!
THE CREATURE HAD A "BLACK BOX" FASTENED
TO ITS WAIST AND MOTIONED FOR THE MEN
TO COME CLOSER. A DOCTOR, A MAYOR
AND POLICE ARE ALL CONVINCED THE
MEN ARE TELLING THE TRUTH!

ITEM:

June, 1947. Washington State: Idaho pilot and businessman Kenneth Arnold claimed he saw nine discs flying in formation near his plane over the mountains of Washington State. He described the undulating motion of each disc as "like a saucer skipping over water." This description reinforced the use of the term "flying saucer" in UFO terminology. The U.S. Air Force investigated Arnold and his claims thoroughly and could arrive at no explanation for the sightings. This incident was among the first of a post-World War II wave of UFO reports.

SEVERAL BIZARRE EVENTS *TERRIFIED* THE
CAST AND CREW OF "CLOSE ENCOUNTERS"
WHILE THE FILM WAS BEING MADE. _UNEXPLAINED
CLOUDS, SUDDEN STORMS_ AND OTHER _STRANGE
HAPPENINGS_ MADE MANY CAST MEMBERS THINK
THAT SOME *FORCE* DID _NOT_ WANT THE FILM TO
BE MADE!

ITEM:

Late evening, October 26, 1958. Baltimore, Maryland: Two men were driving toward a bridge that crossed the Loch Raven Reservoir near Baltimore. While driving, they saw a highly illuminated object which they described as "large, flat and sort of egg-shaped, hanging between 100 and 150 feet off the top of the superstructure of the bridge over the lake." As they drove closer to the bridge, their car's dashboard lights, headlights, and engine failed, and the ignition did not work. The two men then watched the UFO for a little over half a minute, and then saw a great flash of light and heard a loud noise. The object then began to rise rapidly and disappeared within five to ten seconds. Several other people later claimed that they had also seen a strange light in the area of the bridge that evening.

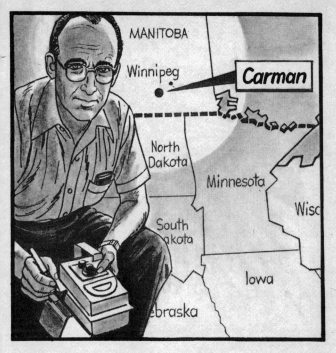

FOUR MASSIVE <u>RINGS OF RADIATION</u>... ABOUT 50 FEET IN DIAMETER... ARE CAUSED BY **UFO**S, ACCORDING TO ERNEST SPIELMAN OF THE MANITOBA MUSEUM OF MAN AND NATURE. THE RINGS ARE IN MANITOBA, CANADA... ALSO THE AREA OF <u>MANY UFO SIGHTINGS</u>! IS THIS THE LANDING BASE FOR VISITORS FROM OUTER SPACE?

"BIGFOOT" MAY BE A CREATURE FROM OUTER SPACE!

IN JULY, 1974, DOZENS OF WITNESSES SAW A UFO CRASH INTO LAKE OKEECHOBEE IN THE FLORIDA SWAMPLAND. SIX MONTHS LATER, A SECURITY GUARD AT A HOUSING DEVELOPMENT SITE SAID HE SHOT SIX BULLETS AT A HUGE, HAIRY AND VERY SMELLY MONSTER!

ITEM:
April 17, 1966. Shortly after 5:00 AM: Two members of the Portage County, Ohio, sheriff's office spied a UFO hovering only about 100 feet in the air over a wooded area. The two men, Deputy Sheriff Dale Spaur and Deputy Wilbur Neff, described the object as being shaped like an ice cream cone, about 25 to 35 feet in diameter, and highly illuminated. The men chased the UFO and were soon joined by another patrol car 40 miles east, near East Palentine, Ohio. The two cars then pursued the object another 30 miles across the state line to Conway, Pennsylvania. There they stopped near the parked state police patrol car of Officer Frank Panzanella. All four men then observed the UFO rise rapidly to about 3,500 feet, stop momentarily, and finally continue to ascend as it disappeared.

ITEM:
January 11, 1977. Night: A silent gleaming UFO was observed by two Tennessee law officers for over ten minutes. It streaked across the sky of four counties—and then vanished!

AT LEAST 30 *DIFFERENT TYPES OF UFOs* HAVE BEEN
SEEN BY PEOPLE THROUGHOUT THE WORLD. THEIR SHAPES
RANGE FROM THE POPULAR "SAUCERS"...TO TOPS...GLOBES
...CIGARS... *EVEN ONE SHAPED LIKE A LIGHT BULB.*

WHAT DOES A FLYING SAUCER LOOK LIKE?

Flying saucers don't always look like saucers. In fact, they come in many shapes, sizes, and colors judging from reports on record. They can be disc-shaped, can resemble torpedoes and cigars, jellyfish, or be top-shaped. They can be red, orange, green, bright blue, yellow, or white, and sometimes they change colors during flight.

A UFO that looked like a Christmas tree was sighted in Monticello, Wisconsin, on April 3, 1964. The object reminded the young professor and his family of a Christmas tree because most of the lights were green, red, and white.

Sixty percent of the UFOs reported seen on the ground have a diameter of between two and five meters (or six to fifteen feet). On the other hand, objects reported in continuous flight are usually described as having diameters of fifteen to thirty meters (or sixty to one hundred feet). Does that mean that UFOs can change their size when they are in the air—or when they are on the ground?

Of one thing we can be certain about UFOs— any visitors to our planet are not likely to call our sun their home!

Near Earth, the hull of a space ship will register at about 65°F. Past Venus, which is 67 million miles from the sun, the temperature would reach 160°F. Within 10 million miles of the sun the temperature would zoom to 1,000°F. From 5 million miles out, 2,000°F. And one million miles from the sun our space ship's hull would register 4,500°F!

The
Sun

The strongest power source known to man is the sun's radiation—or sunlight. Its output is tremendous—with a horsepower measured at 500,000,-000,000,000,000,000,000! Much of this power is diluted by the time it reaches the Earth.

The sun has been described as an amazingly complex nuclear powerhouse releasing stupendous amounts of energy. The sun transforms 564 million tons of hydrogen into helium *every second!* It also converts to energy four million tons of hydrogen every second at a temperature of 13 million degrees Celsius. This constant transformation of matter, enabling the sun to expend a regular rate of energy and sending fountains of flame thousands of miles into space, has been going on for approximately five billion years!

ONLY SEEN DURING AN ECLIPSE!

Two layers of the sun, the corolla and the chromosphere, can only be observed when the moon is blocking the light from the sun during a total or near-total eclipse.

During a total solar eclipse the moon passes between the sun and the earth and blocks all of the sun's rays from some regions of the earth. The last total solar eclipse in the United States occurred on March 7, 1970 and lasted three minutes. The next solar eclipse visible from the United States will occur in 1979.

THE FIVE PARTS OF THE SUN

No, the sun is not just one big ball of fire. It's actually made up of five very different parts. In the center is the core, the sun's generating plant. Next to the core is the sun's energy-transporting area. Beyond this is the sun's photosphere, the only area that we can always see with the naked eye. Two other outside areas—the chromosphere and the corona—can only be seen during a total eclipse!

All but one of the chemical elements we know today were first found on the Earth. In 1869 the English astronomer Lockyer, while studying the sun, discovered an element unknown on Earth— and called it helium! Later helium was also discovered here. Somewhat less than half of the sun's content is pure helium and half is pure hydrogen. A very small amount of various other elements comprise the rest. In short, the sun is just a bunch of hot air!

How hot? That depends on where you stand. On the sun's surface, the temperature is a mere 6,000°C. But in the center it climbs to 20 million degrees! Astronomers who study the sun have found that they become uncomfortably hot even in their special solar observatories. To solve this problem, they've begun to reflect the sun's image down into an underground room, where it can be studied at a more comfortable temperature!

We know that our sun is an average-sized, middle-aged star, about 4.6 billion years old. Like all stars, our sun began as a huge sphere of gases. Compacted by its own gravity it grew so hot that a continuous nuclear reaction began at the center. These nuclear fires extend millions of miles from the center in all directions.

The Greek astronomer Xenophanes, born 570 B.C., thought that the sun was replaced every morning. He also believed that the sun, moon and stars were actually flaming clouds.

MANY PEOPLE WHO HAVE HAD CONTACT WITH UFOs HAVE GOTTEN STRANGE, UNEXPLAINED SUNBURNS!

THE <u>YOUNGEST</u> PERSON EVER TO BE
TAKEN ABOARD A FLYING SAUCER IS
<u>A 15-YEAR OLD BOY</u> FROM BROWNSTOWN,
ILLINOIS.

Anaxagoras (c. 500 B.C.) was a Greek teacher who first discovered the cause of eclipses. He was forced into exile from his native Athens for daring to claim that the sun was larger than the Peloponnesus peninsula (the land of Greece)!

$$\frac{SUN}{EARTH} = ?$$

Just how much larger is the sun than the Earth? While its diameter is only 100 times that of Earth, its density is approximately 333,000 times greater than the Earth's mass. And if you'd care to visualize the distance from the Earth to the sun—93 million miles—try this. Just imagine traveling the distance of the Earth's diameter . . . 10,000 times!

If the sun were a large pumpkin, the Earth would be the size of a pea, the moon the size of a poppy seed, and New York's World Trade Center would barely be a speck of dust!

HE NEVER KNEW WHAT HE SAW!

Even great astronomers can blow it! Looking at the sun through a home-made screen, Johannes Kepler saw what he thought was the planet Mercury in front of it. Satisfied, Kepler quit for the day —and missed his chance to discover sunspots!

TWO BRITISH ASTRONOMERS HAVE COME
UP WITH A _NEW THEORY_ OF FLU AND
COLDS. SIR FRED HOYLE AND CHANDRA
WICKRAMASINGHE, PROFESSORS AT
UNIVERSITY COLLEGE IN CARDIFF, WALES,
BELIEVE THAT OUR "BUGS" ARE ACTUALLY
CAUSED _BY COMETS FROM OUTER_ SPACE!

HOW MANY SPOTS DOES OUR SUN HAVE?

Scientists have observed that the sun's spots run in cycles. Some years, the sun will have only fifty groups of sunspots—at other times the sunspots increase to an annual rate of over 500 groups! In 1947 one of these groups of sunspots covered an area 2,000 million square miles!

You've heard of shooting stars? Well, our sun is one of those, too. Only what it shoots is part of its own matter. These eruptions, called prominences, sometimes reach lengths of hundreds of thousands of miles.

SUNWARD, HO!

On December 10, 1974 Germany launched its Helios-1 spacecraft. The probe came closer to the sun than any previous spacecraft—28 million miles!

How close to the sun could a manned spaceship approach safely? Pretty close, if it's done correctly. There is a minor planet named Icarus which comes within 17 million miles of the sun every 13 months. This rocky little planet is only one to two miles in diameter and has a surface temperature of 1,000°F. Its best feature is its large conical shadow, a shadow which a spaceship could use to shield itself from the extreme temperatures of the sun.

Four billion years from now the sun will probably have become several times brighter. This may cause Earth's oceans to boil and our atmosphere to fill with carbon dioxide. Mars' temperature could rise from 100°F below zero to an average of 70°F above!

Scientists expect that our sun will eventually use up the last of its "nuclear fuel"—and then explode! How much longer do we have to go? Just another six billion years!

The
Planets

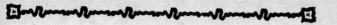

The nine major and millions of minor objects that revolve around the sun comprise the solar system. These nine planets all circle the sun in the same direction. All but Pluto are on virtually the same plane. Mercury is the closest planet to the sun—if you call 36 million miles away close!

MERCURY

The possibility of life on Mercury, the planet closest to the sun, is very unlikely because there is no air or water. The temperature on the sunny side rises to 700-800°F, while on the dark side the temperature plummets to 400°F below zero.

The diameter of Mercury is 3,000 miles, as opposed to Mars' 4,200 miles. Both planets, however, have the same surface gravity. Thus, an astronaut exploring Mars or Mercury would weigh the same—roughly 38% of what he would weigh on Earth.

With the use of new types of equipment scientists were amazed to discover that Mercury behaves in a manner totally different from what they once believed. They found that Mercury completes a rotation on its own axis in approximately 59 days, which is much less than the 88 days it takes Mercury to revolve about the sun. Thus, the old notion that Mercury receives radiation from the sun on no more than ½ its surface was found to be false.

Being closer to the sun than Earth, Mercury circles the sun in less time than Earth—one fourth the time. A year on Mercury only lasts 88 days. If that weren't reason enough not to spend your summer vacation there, the heat would be—it reaches over 1,300°F!

VENUS

Our closest neighbor is Venus—which, at one point, is only 25 million miles away! Unfortunately, because it has its back to us then, it is almost invisible.

Venus possesses an unusual characteristic: it rotates clockwise—or just the opposite of all the other planets! Since it rotates once every 243 days, which is longer than the time it takes to revolve about the sun, then once every 117 Earth days the sun rises in the West on Venus!

SUNSET ON VENUS

On Venus, light rays are curved at a *180° angle!* This means you can see the sun set—even with your back to it! However, the distortion of the horizon is so great that you seem to be standing at the bottom of a *super-large bowl!*

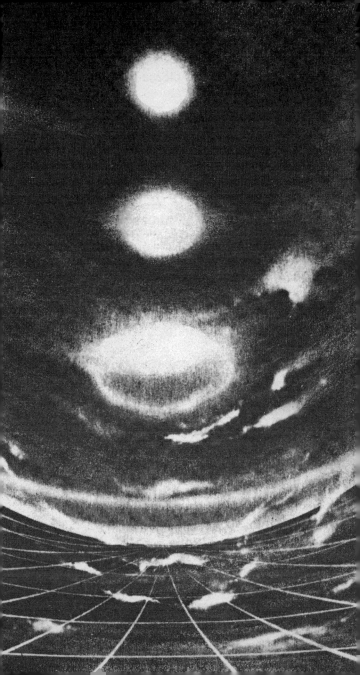

Could there be life on Venus? Probably not. Its climate is the most unpleasant in the solar system, with extreme temperatures, crushing pressures, noxious and corrosive gases, sulfurous smells, and a gloomy landscape. Not even a Greek goddess could live there!

How hot does it get on Venus? Hot enough to melt tin and lead! Although Venus is 67 million miles from the sun the surface temperature is 900-1000°F. Its surface seethes with glowing lava and molten metal. The carbon dioxide atmosphere creates a "greenhouse effect" by trapping solar radiation, thus causing temperatures to rise to such high levels. This cloud cover makes it impossible for us on Earth to see the surface of Venus, our closest planetary neighbor.

Venus's clouds also contain enormous quantities of sulphuric acid, hydrochloric acid, and hydrofluoric acid. A spacecraft landing on Venus would disintegrate almost immediately—unless it had heavy, super-strong armor protection.

How can we change the planet Venus? Some scientists have suggested seeding the clouds of Venus with algae. They say the algae would change carbon dioxide and water into carbohydrates and oxygen. This process would also reduce the total pressure, decrease the infra-red light, and lower the temperature—and might even make Venus habitable!

MARS

The planet Mars was the key to an important discovery. Observing the planet carefully, astronomer Johannes Kepler found that its orbit was not a perfect circle. From this he deduced that the gravitational force of the sun controlled the planet's orbit! What's more, Kepler made his observations without the aid of a telescope!

Radio waves travel at 186,000 miles a second. If you were conversing with a friend on Mars, it would take him 3½ minutes to receive your message and vice-versa.

Mars, the red planet, really *is* red! In fact, color photographs taken by the Viking I spacecraft after landing on Mars show that even the atmosphere is a rosy red color! It was also revealed in these photographs that the surface of Mars, like our moon, has many craters.

Another surprising result of the Viking photographs is the evidence that there were ancient floods of water, indicated by erosion patterns and the snaking paths of dried river beds. Most of the water from these rivers either evaporated into space or froze beneath the Martian surface centuries ago. These long-gone rivers have no connection with the mythical "canals" supposed by 19th-century astronomers to exist on Mars.

Mars is the only planet that regularly changes its color! At the top of this red sphere is a white polar cap which scientists think may be either frost or frozen carbon dioxide. When this cap becomes smaller during the Martian summer, a dark-brown tint comes over much of the red areas. As

EARTH,

This spectacular sight based on actual photographs taken from outer space shows the Earth, Mars and the Moon, in quarter phase, in proportion to true size.

MOON

MARS,

the Martian winter approaches, this brown area then fades as the cap becomes larger!

Are there Martians on Mars—little green men? For many years this planet, along with Venus and Mercury, held the promise of life, but the first close-up photos of Mars revealed a planet marked with craters and resembling our moon. However, when the Viking lander arrived on Mars in 1976, it was found that those craters were only on one side of Mars. The other side was more like the Earth—covered with volcanoes, a desert-like environment on the red planet's Plain of Chryse, canyons, and signs of erosion by huge rivers. Those rivers may be dry now, but once they held water—and where there is water, there could be life!

The Martian air is so light that it's similar to what exists at 100,000 feet on Earth. Without a pressure suit, man could not exist. The air pressure on Mars is so low that a plane could not fly! And that's not all . . . Mars doesn't have enough oxygen to operate a jet engine. Even a parachute would collapse on the red planet unless it moved at a tremendous speed.

Blue sky? Not on Mars! The Martian sky is orange!

The largest volcano on Mars, Mount Olympus, has a 300-mile cone of lava at the base and is nearly 70,000 feet high. It is twice as large and twice as high as the largest volcanoes on Earth.

The presence of volcanoes on Mars may mean there was life on the red planet, since volcanoes need water to develop. Water also provides the fluid in which the basic molecules of the living cell can drift about and collide, thus creating more complex organisms.

Both of Mars' moons are less than twenty miles in diameter. It takes Mars and its two small moons 687 days to circle the sun. Deimos, one of the two Martian moons, has a revolution period of 30 days, which fairly approximates the Martian day. Because of this similarity, Deimos always appears to be racing Mars—and always manages to barely lose the race! Phobos, Mars' second moon, is the most unusual in our solar system! Every time Mars rotates on its axis, Phobos completes three revolutions. Because of this, you can see Phobos rising in the west and setting in the east—from the surface of Mars, of course.

Scientists have discovered that Phobos has a decaying orbit. This led a Russian astronomer, I. S. Shklovskii, to suggest that Phobos and its sister moon Deimos are actually artificial satellites, sent into space by a highly advanced Martian civilization!

Want to play baseball on Phobos? Alone? Here's how to do it. Pitch the ball to the horizon at a speed of 20 to 30 miles per hour. Then go home for lunch. After a few hours, return, pick up a bat, face the other direction and await the pitch. If you miss the ball, go home for another 2 hours and return with a catcher's mitt. But if you hit the ball, still go home for 2 hours, but return with a fielder's mitt. There's only one problem with this game: daylight on Phobos only lasts 4 hours!

JUPITER

The solar system's largest planet, Jupiter, is well over 1,300 times larger than Earth! It is also 100 times its area. If Earth were superimposed across the face of Jupiter, it would be about the size of India. The planet Jupiter takes twelve of our years to revolve around the sun—but is goes through a complete Jovian day in only nine hours and 51 minutes!

The most distinctive visible feature of Jupiter is the Great Red Spot, which is evidently a 300-year-old storm center with a surface area greater than that of the entire Earth! That storm must pack quite a wallop!

In some ways, Jupiter is more like an incomplete star than a giant planet. Jupiter has no surface. It is a ball of hydrogen and helium not quite hot enough to ignite. Yet Jupiter gives off 2½ times more heat into space than it gets from the sun, 483 million miles away.

On January 7, 1610, Galileo was watching the planet Jupiter when he saw several bright stars near it. Observing these same "stars" in different positions over the next few nights, he discovered the four "stars" were really Jupiter's moons!

When we look at the planet Jupiter, we actually see groups of cloud belts, which move faster at Jupiter's equator than they do at its poles. Many spots—including the constant "red spot"—appear on these clouds, and scientists are still not sure what they are.

Jupiter is no place to begin a diet, as it has a surface gravity 2.65 times greater than that of Earth. A person with an Earth weight of 200 pounds would weigh 530 pounds when standing

AN ENDLESS FURY OF WIND
The *large* bands on the surface of Jupiter are thought to be *constantly moving clouds*—carrying with them gusts of wind as *fierce as earth's tropical storms!* And the great planet's huge *Red Spot* is itself believed to be a gigantic *hurricane!*

on Jupiter! To escape the gravitational pull of Earth, a space ship has to go 36,700 feet per second. To break Jupiter's gravitational pull, the space ship would require a speed of 200,000 feet per second.

Jupiter's atmosphere is only 50 miles deep. To enter its atmosphere, we would need a bathyscaphe instead of a space ship because a space ship couldn't land on its surface. Why? Because the atmosphere is so thick! If it did land, it would sink!

In spite of its enormous size, Jupiter is not all that heavy. As it is made up almost entirely of gases, its density is only 1.3 times that of water!

Of all the planets in our solar system, Jupiter may be the only other planet having life forms. It has a density only a fourth that of Earth and possesses essentially similar materials of dust and clouds from which the solar system was created. It is conceivable that Jupiter has a variety of life forms, since its atmosphere is much like primitive Earth's—hydrogen, methane, ammonia, and water.

Scientists have recently discovered that something is sending out radio waves—from the planet Jupiter! No one yet knows why these waves occur —but they are not connected to any of the planet's surface features!

SATURN

The planet Saturn covers an area 700 times greater than Earth, but has a density of only 95 times that of our planet. Why? Because Saturn, with its mixture of hydrogen and methane, has a lower mass than water!

Scientists believe that *Saturn's rings*—fragments of rock and ice—might have become *moons* if they had been farther away from the planet!

Could there be life on Saturn, Uranus, or Neptune? Because of their composition, these planets resemble the sun more than the Earth. Although they probably contain the molecular components of living matter, their unearthlike environments make it seem unlikely that these will ever evolve into more complex forms of life.

If Saturn were plunged into an enormous sea, the whole planet would float! That's because Saturn's low density of only .68 is about that of a milkshake!

The second-largest moon in our solar system belongs to Saturn. This moon, Titan, is 3,500 miles in diameter—almost half the size of Earth! Shortly after discovering Jupiter's four moons, Galileo thought he saw two moons around Saturn. Saturn's "moons," however, didn't act the way moons were supposed to, and Galileo was never able to solve their mystery. A more powerful telescope would have revealed the planet's rings. Except for having the rings and only ten moons, Saturn is a somewhat smaller and more distant version of Jupiter.

Saturn's rings have a diameter of 170,000 miles, but are only 10 miles thick! The three rings are kept from merging into each other by the pull of Saturn's ten moons—and the space between the first and second ring is around 1,700 miles! What are they made of? Scientists think it's frozen ammonia!

URANUS

Sir William Herschel, an observational astronomer, discovered the planet Uranus in 1781.

Significantly, this was the first planet to be discovered telescopically! Uranus has a diameter of 29,600 miles and is *1,783 million miles* from the sun! It is so far away that the rings, like Saturn's, weren't discovered until 1977 . . . and then it was by accident!

Because of this vast distance, the average temperature on Uranus is 210° C (or 310°F) *below zero* . . . hardly the ideal spot to spend your summer vacation.

The tremendous distance from the sun also means that it takes Uranus 84 years to orbit the sun!

One of the strangest characteristics of Uranus concerns its orbit. Most planets rotate on an axis which is almost perpendicular to their orbiting plane. Uranus, however, rotates on an axis almost in the same plane as its orbit plane—98° to it! As

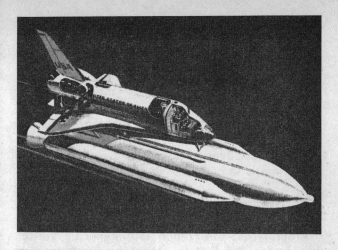

THE SUPER SHUTTLE

Want to scoot about between *planets?* You may soon be able to—in this new Space Shuttle. This amazing craft weighs *170,000 pounds,* is *122 feet long* and has a *78-foot wing span.* In other words, it's about the size of a DC-9 jet! And it can carry up to *65,000 pounds!*

a result, its poles and its equator alternately face the sun.

Uranus has five satellites and it was, in fact, the somewhat disturbed motion of these satellites, which appear to follow no rule in the direction in which they orbit, which hinted that there must be another planet beyond. These slight irregularities led to the discovery of Neptune, the eighth planet to be named to our solar system.

NEPTUNE

Around 1843 the French astronomer Le Verrier was among the first to notice the discrepancies of the orbits of Uranus' moons. Le Verrier proposed the notion of a planet beyond and in 1846 a German astronomer, Galle, was able to confirm Le Verrier's belief.

Neptune is considerably farther than Uranus, at a distance of 2,790 million miles from the sun. One orbit takes 165 years! With a diameter of 27,700 miles, Neptune has a density 2.2 times that of water and its temperature never rises above 230°C below zero!

One of Neptune's two moons is so eccentric that its orbiting distance from the planet varies from one million miles to six million miles!

PLUTO

It was in the first years of the 20th century that scientists discovered the small changes in the orbits of Saturn and Uranus, as well as unexplained movements in certain groups of comets. Percival Lowell published his belief that even beyond Neptune there must be a new planet. In 1914 he even predicted its position, but he couldn't find it. An American astronomer, Clyde Tombaugh, was to claim the honors in 1930. Pluto is appropriately named after the god of the underworld and, at 4,000 miles across, is so small—perhaps too small to cause the irregularities in the behavior of other planets with which it is credited—that many scientists believe there may yet be a tenth, as yet undiscovered, planet.

At an average distance of 3,670,000,000 miles from our sun, is Pluto the farthest planet? Well, most of the time, yes. But because of the high

THE COLDEST PLANET IN THE SOLAR SYSTEM? ...IT'S PLUTO! THE SURFACE TEMPERATURE IS 420°F BELOW ZERO...OR JUST 39°F ABOVE ABSOLUTE ZERO —THE COLDEST POSSIBLE TEMPERATURE! WHEN IT'S THAT COLD, NITROGEN FREEZES.

irregularity of its orbit, Pluto's cigar-shaped path often crosses that of Neptune, its closest neighbor. This puts Pluto closer to the sun than Neptune for about 1/6 of its orbit. Fortunately, the two bodies have not yet collided in their attempts not to be last!

Pluto is so far from the sun that its temperature is 420°F *below zero,* and one trip around the sun (365 days for the Earth) takes Pluto two and a half centuries!

Life on Pluto? This planet is at the outer edge of the solar system. It may have an Earth-like composition, but since it is so far from the sun it's probably a frozen, silent world, too cold to support life.

The
Earth

The Earth is the third planet from the sun, at a distance of almost 93 million miles. The Earth is the closest planet to the sun to have a moon. And our moon is about as different from the Earth as it could be. The moon's surface is scarred with millions of craters, the result of collisions with small asteroids. The Earth would have many such scars as well, but asteroids burn up in our atmosphere and seldom strike the Earth's surface.

Who was the first man to say that the Earth is round? Aristotle. But nobody would believe him. Even though he was a famous Greek philosopher, people thought he was a fool when it came to his book entitled *About Heaven.* They wondered how the people living at the antipodes (to us, Australians) could walk upside down without falling off the Earth. This argument against Aristotle persisted for 2,000 years, into the 15th century. Even Columbus was not sure that he wouldn't fall off the Earth. It was not until Magellan that the last doubt about the spherical shape of the Earth finally disappeared.

Another who believed the Earth to be round was Pythagoras, who created a club whose members were forbidden to poke an iron bar into a fire or eat beans!

Though he had no advanced instruments, the Greek astronomer Eratosthenes was the first person to accurately measure the Earth's circumference. How did he do it? Simple. He recorded the degrees of the sun's position at high noon over the towns of Alexandria and Syene, discovered the distances between them, and then calculated the additional miles needed to make the Earth's circumference equal to 360°, or a complete circle.

Most people think Copernicus was the first person to say that the Earth moves around the sun. But they're wrong . . . the Greek scientist Aristarchus did so, 1800 years earlier!

Do you feel dizzy? If so, no wonder! Did you know that as you are reading this item you are hurtling around the sun at the speed of 70,000 miles per hour?

The astronomer Ptolemy didn't believe the Earth could rotate. If it did, he thought, there would be a constant, howling wind. But the Earth does rotate on its axis once every 24 hours, right? Well, not exactly. Astronomical measurements of the Earth's rotation from 1750 to 1917 revealed that the Earth constantly lost or gained several seconds every few years. By 1960, the Earth's timing was off by 33 seconds.

Since 1967 our time has been measured by the use of an atom (or Caesium) clock. Its advantages are two: it doesn't depend on mechanics and its accuracy level is almost perfect—only a one-second deviation every 300 years!

The use of calendars to record time is not at all a recent development; almost 5,000 years ago the Chinese developed a calendar that had *365 days!*

Copernicus

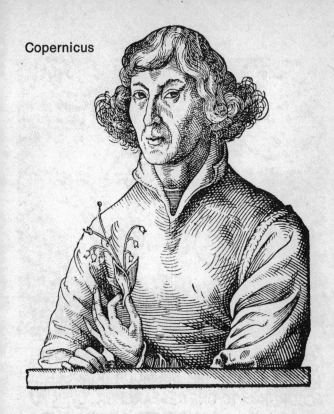

The Chinese also were the first to build and use sundials!

The prehistoric Mayans were superlative astronomers. They predicted eclipses with amazing precision and developed a calendar that is in many ways superior to the one we use today.

Ever wonder how to get more vacation into your year? Just follow the pattern of the ancient Egyptians. Although their calendar was similar to ours, they chose to give each month only 30 days—leaving five extra days per year!

THE GREAT LAKES TRIANGLE IS MORE **DEADLY** THAN THE BERMUDA TRIANGLE... ACCORDING TO ONE RESEARCHER. <u>OVER</u> **70** INCIDENTS OF **ACCIDENTS, DEATHS AND UNEXPLAINED EVENTS** HAVE BEEN RECORDED IN THE TRAGIC AREA *!*

SCIENTISTS ARE BAFFLED BY STRANGE, POWER-
FUL X-RAYS THAT APPEARED ON OCT. 28, 1970...
AND DID NOT DISAPPEAR FOR 2 MONTHS! THESE X-
RAYS WERE POWERFUL ENOUGH TO REACH TO
OUTER SPACE...AND WERE DETECTED BY SEV-
ERAL SATELLITES! WHERE DID THEY COME
FROM? *THE MIDDLE OF THE SO. ATLANTIC!*

In Jules Verne's "Journey to the Center of the Earth" his hero enters a cave and embarks upon a series of adventures. But it's far more likely that on penetrating the Earth one would find only molten rocks, because the Earth's temperature increases at the rate of 30°C per kilometer (or 16°F per thousand feet). At that rate, the Earth's temperature reaches the melting point of rocks (1200-1800°C) at only 50 kilometers beneath the surface. And the 1% of solid crust upon which Earthlings find it comfortable to live must have begun forming several billion years ago—because it takes that long for molten rocks to cool!

How deep is this 1% which is actually used to support life? Not very! The Earth's core, mantle, and crust have a combined radius of almost 4,000 miles—yet the soil we use to grow our crops is only a few feet thick! This shallow layer, however, contains clues to numerous questions that scientists relentlessly study. Through what we find on the Earth's very surface many answers may be revealed, and even more questions raised . . .

The Earth's oldest rocks have been found in Karelia, in Finland, and in the Black Hills of South Dakota.

In 1885, a polished metal cylinder—seemingly man-made—was found embedded in a vein of Pennsylvania coal formed over 12 million years ago!

An unusual gold artifact has been found in the Andes of South America. Archaeologists say it was crafted between the years of 800 and 900 A.D. *Yet* it clearly seems to be the image of a modern, swept-wing jet!

Mysterious lines, known as the Nazca Lines, are

MEXICAN CAVE DRAWINGS – *OVER 1,500 YRS. OLD!* – ARE INCREDIBLY LIKE DRAWINGS FOUND IN AUSTRALIA AND NORTH AFRICA. *ALL THREE REVEAL THE SAME VISITORS FROM ANOTHER PLANET!*

THE IMPOSSIBLE MAP

Sometime between 1513 and 1520 A.D. a Turkish admiral named Muhuddin Piri Reis compiled a map from charts of unknown origin. When the Reis map was re-discovered on November 8, 1929 it was found to be astonishingly accurate!

Further investigation showed an ice-free Antarctic Ocean—something that could not have existed when Reis made his map! What's more, Reis' map was so detailed, it could only have been made from the air! Where Reis got all this information is still a mystery to experts. Some think the map must have been made by a highly sophisticated civilization, thousands of years before the ice age!

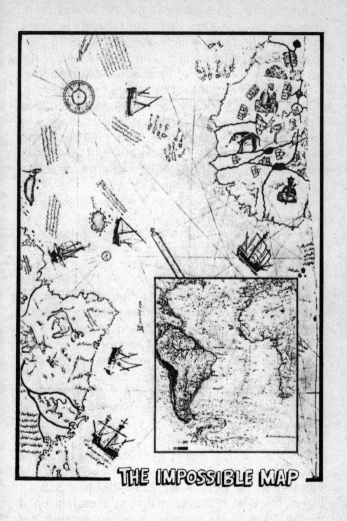

THE IMPOSSIBLE MAP

located on a high plateau in the Peruvian desert. They are broad yellow lines cut through the dark soil to the underlying light-colored subsoil. They appear meaningless when seen from ground level, but from the air the lines—some are 40 miles long —depict animals, insects, flowers, and strange, half-human, half-godlike creatures. Modern dating techniques have shown that the lines were laid down between the years 400 and 1200 A.D. Who designed them? Why? And who would have seen those astonishing drawings, at least five centuries before the invention of the airplane?

At first glance, the Earth's upper atmosphere seems to be uninviting. All of our weather and almost 90% of our air comes from the lower atmosphere, so why bother about what's further up? In the first place, the upper atmosphere's ozone layer shields us from the sun's excess radiation. But that's not all. It also protects us from meteors . . . makes radio communication possible . . . and gives us the auroras borealis and australus.

In ancient times, it wasn't known that auroras were caused by particles from the solar wind caught in the magnetic field of the Earth's upper atmosphere. The Greeks thought them to be fires in the sky, while a 13th-century Norseman thought they were caused by the ice radiating the light it had absorbed during the day.

In April, 1902, a theory held for many centuries was refuted by French scientist Leon Philippe Teisserenc de Bort. After 236 individual balloon flights, de Bort discovered that at a certain point in the Earth's atmosphere, the temperature not only stabilized, it actually increased!

"*SILENT SOUND WAVES*" ARE POWER-
FUL ENOUGH TO DESTROY SHIPS AND
PLANES!

CLOUDS

There are clouds, called noctilucent clouds, moving about the Earth, 250,000 feet above the surface. They sweep over the Earth in a near-vacuum at a height of 50 miles at speeds of up to 400 miles per hour! At that height the air is much thinner even than that on the surface of Mars! Most interesting of all are the unique characteristics of these clouds:

- they undulate
- they sometimes appear to hover motionless
- parts of a particular cloud move in one direction while parts of the same cloud move in the opposite direction!

On March 22, 1870, the sailors of the *Lady of the Lake* saw a strange cloud in the sky. They reported to their captain who recorded in his log book a small diagram of this remarkable phenomenon. It was light gray in color, like a cloud, but was lower than other clouds and moved from 20° above the horizon to 80° above—and it traveled *against* the wind!

ENOUGH **HOT DOGS** ARE PRODUCED IN
THE U.S. **EVERY YEAR** TO REACH THE
MOON AND BACK 2½ TIMES!

METEORS/METEORITES

About 1,000 tons of meteor dust falls onto the Earth every single day. This is because the Earth collides with about 100 million shooting stars and uncounted billions of micrometeorites every day!

Shooting stars are normally invisible. Only when they touch the Earth's upper atmosphere do we see these meteors.

Lights appeared in the sky over Bloomington, Indiana on the evening of September 7, 1877. Many people supposed them to be meteors. They appeared and disappeared at intervals of every three or four seconds. After a while, there was darkness for several minutes, followed by a final flash of light. No explanations have ever been given.

Over the last 130 years, meteorites have struck at least 15 buildings in locations as diverse as New York, Finland, and Australia. Thus far, no one has been hurt!

The "Ozark Fireball" was one of the most spectacular meteors ever photographed. It appeared over Oklahoma, Kansas, and Missouri on October 9, 1969, and was so brilliant that its light was tracked nearly 400 miles away at Urbana, Illinois. The Ozark Fireball penetrated the Earth's atmosphere to within 15 miles, causing sonic booms over a vast area. It then exploded suddenly—and completely disappeared!

In January, 1916, an unexplained shock hit the city of Cincinnati, Ohio, and caused buildings to shake. The blast followed a strange explosion in the sky, from which flashes were seen.

THE LARGEST METEORITE EVER FOUND ON
EARTH FELL IN 1920 AT HOBA WEST IN SOUTHWEST
AFRICA. IT WAS **NINE FEET** BY **EIGHT FEET**
AND WEIGHED *132,000 POUNDS!*

EXPLOSIONS FROM THE SKY!

On October 25, 1889 in the town of Chesham, about 25 miles northeast of Reading in England, several flocks of sheep broke from their folds and ran in common alarm over a region of thirty square miles.

The only plausible explanation is that this occurred shortly after meteoric explosions in the sky.

What happens when a meteor hits the Earth?
Because the friction from impact is so strong, a meteor usually melts. Not only that, it also leaves a large, deep crater in the Earth's surface. One such crater, the Great Crater of Arizona, has a depth of 600 feet and a diameter of almost a mile!

The largest "star wound" on Earth's surface is the Vredefort Ring in Transvaal, South Africa. Its dome is over 26 miles wide. The Vredefort Ring is believed to be over a quarter of a billion years old.

On June 30, 1908, an explosion more powerful than an atomic bomb rocked Siberia. Eyewitnesses reported seeing a ball of fire and towering cloud of smoke. Trees for dozens of miles around were flattened by the shock waves. In 1927 a scientific expedition sent to the site found no evidence that it was caused by a meteor. What was it then? A collision between the Earth and "anti-matter" from outer space of another sort perhaps? Alexander Kazantsev, a distinguished metallurgist, says all evidence points to the explosion of a giant airborne craft. The year 1908 was just five years after the Wright brothers made their first flight.

ASTEROIDS AND COMETS

There are large deposits of metal floating around in space in the form of meteorites and asteroids. With only one asteroid 300 yards in diameter the world's iron supply for at least one year could be met!

The biggest asteroid is Ceres! With a diameter of 480 miles and a surface area of 700,000 square miles, Ceres is as large as all the United States Confederate States put together!

The ancients considered comets a sign of impending disaster. The appearance of a comet in the sky would fill their hearts with dread. In reality a comet is just a dirty snowball in space! It's nothing but ice, frozen gasses, and bits of meteoric rock.

Comets "come alive" when they are 300 million miles from the sun and the sun's radiation heats the comet's nucleus. By the time the comet is within 100 million miles of the sun, the huge tail of the comet is created. Some of these tails have lengths of 200 million miles. In 1910 the tail of Halley's Comet passed through the Earth's atmosphere with no harmful effects—although disaster was expected!

It is estimated that there are more than 100 million comets that go around our sun. Less than 100 comets perform a complete revolution of the sun within a hundred years. About 40 to 50 of them have orbits of 100 to 1,000 years.

Most of the comets in our solar system have such a long journey that we can never know when they'll pass our way. The exception, of course, is Halley's Comet, first discovered in 1682, which visits us every 76 years!

In 1975, our earth was treated to the astonishingly *brilliant* display of *Comet West*. The tail of this comet was in the shape of a *beautiful fan!*

THERE ARE OVER <u>4,000</u> MAN-MADE THINGS FLYING ABOUT IN <u>OUTER SPACE!</u>

EVEN THE SCIENTISTS WHO SENT THEM UP THERE HAVE LOST TRACK OF THEM. ONE BRITISH SATELLITE TRACKER SAYS "WE FIND ONE BIT AND LOSE ANOTHER!"

FROM THE SKY!

Lots of oddities—not all explicable—have landed on the Earth's surface:

ITEM:

1829. Persia: A substance fell from the sky which people said they'd never before seen. They noticed that the sheep ate it and so they ground it into flour and made bread— bread that was attractive-looking but taste-less.

ITEM:

June, 1882. An iron factory foreman in Dubuque, Iowa, found "small living frogs" in-side two large hailstones! There was no logi-cal explanation for this event.

ITEM:

In May, 1907, the Town Council of Remire-mont, France, decided to forbid a religious procession. On May 26 the Abbé Gueniot was called from his studies to look at some hail-stones falling during a storm. The stones had what appeared to be paintings of the Virgin of the Hermits. Over one hundred other peo-ple reported seeing hailstones with pictures of the Virgin Mary!

A SHOWER OF FROGS! A SHOWER OF FROGS FELL ON ANTON WAGNER'S FARM NEAR STIRLING, CONN. ON JULY 31, 1921.

ITEM:

July 4, 1917. About 6:20 P.M. an explosion occurred over the town of Colby, Wisconsin, and a stone fell from the sky. On the same date there occurred a solar eclipse and a luminous object appeared in the skies over France.

ITEM:

March 21, 1922: During a heavy snowstorm in the Alps thousands of exotic insects resembling spiders, caterpillars, and huge ants fell on the slopes and quickly died. Local naturalists were unable to explain the phenomenon. There are records of about a half dozen such incidents in the Alps, most occurring during the end of January. In these instances, insects of different species and gravities fell together. Could these then have been migrations of sorts from some other land? If so, could such migrations explain the apparent capability of animals to predict earthquakes?

ITEM:

February 5, 1783. Calabria, Italy: On this occasion occurred the earliest quake reported, and before the tremors could be felt, "many geese cackled," and the "dogs howled so unbearably they were ordered shot." In the village of Friuli all the cats fled their homes before the quake hit.

The night before the great San Francisco quake in 1906 dogs were barking incessantly.

Dogs, cats, and geese may know more than you would imagine! The U.S. Geological Survey revealed recently that animals have strange powers to detect earthquakes before they happen! No known scientific instrument has ever been able to do that. Scientists admit that they should study animals to get clues as to how and why they predict the quakes! Such studies may also tell us why dogs howl at the moon!

ROCKS FROM THE SKY!

For three weeks during late February and early March of 1922, there were regular reports of rocks "falling from the clouds" in the town of Chico, located in a so-called "earthquake region" of California. This was reported in *The New York Times* and the *San Francisco Chronicle* and they were described as "oval-shaped stones" and "'warm rocks."

An investigation yielded the fact that objects had been falling since July, 1921, but were only first reported in November of that year. The only possible explanation offered was the supposition that someone was firing stones from a catapult. However, no solid proof was ever found for this. The objects had no meteoric characteristics.

The
Moon

Earth has the largest relative moon in the solar system. In other words, our moon is larger in relation to the Earth than is any other moon of this solar system in relation to its mother planet. The moon's surface gravity is 1/6 that of Earth. Therefore, an astronaut with a total of 360 pounds of body weight plus equipment would weigh 60 pounds on the moon and could bound about its surface with ease! It is therefore easier to lift your foot on the moon than it is to bring it down again! The problem of weightlessness was first predicted by the English bishop Francis Godwin—in the year 1638! In his book, *Man in the Moon,* Godwin wrote that his hero, Domingo Gonsales, experienced weightlessness—on a trip to the moon!

HOW HOT IS THE MOON?

The temperatures on the moon range between a nighttime low of 250°F below zero and a daytime high of 225°F above! The moon is 300,000 times dimmer than the sun, yet life in our ocean re-

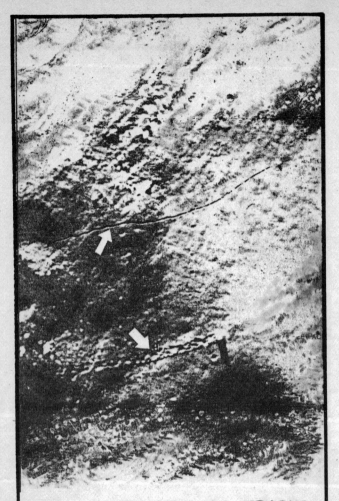

SCIENTISTS HAVE DETECTED **TRACKS ON THE MOON**... PROBABLY MADE BY SOME SPACECRAFT... *IN AREAS THAT WERE <u>NEVER</u> EXPLORED BY* **MAN!**

sponds to the moon's influence—in the form of tides—to a depth of several miles!

The Hughes Aircraft Laboratory in California has developed a highly sensitive "tilt meter." This remarkable device can record lunar tides—even in a cup of tea!

The birth rates of communities on the German coast of the North Sea reveal an astonishing fact. At high tide—when the moon is passing directly overhead—there are an unusually large number of births!

Sir William Lower of Wales—one of the first people to look at the moon through a telescope— described it as looking like a tart. This may have been related to the fact that our moon's surface is riddled with craters.

Ever wonder where the moon's craters come from? Scientists have long wondered how the craters, some of which are over 150 miles across, were originally formed. Most of the craters are believed caused by either meteors or volcanos . . . or both, but nobody really knows for sure.

On May 13, 1972, a huge meteor crashed into the moon. Its impact was equal to about 1,000 tons of TNT. The meteor made a crater as large as a football field on the moon's surface and landed perilously close to the nuclear-powered Apollo-14 science station.

The Mohammedans are the only people using the moon to measure time. A lunar month is 29½ days and twelve lunar months equal a lunar year. Since a lunar year is only 354 days, if you decide to plant according to a lunar calendar on the first

IN 1971, ALAN SHEPARD WAS THE FIRST MAN TO PLAY GOLF ON THE MOON!

THE ASTRONAUT SMUGGLED A SIX-IRON AND A PACK OF BALLS ONTO HIS APOLLO XIV SPACE-CRAFT. ONE SHOT WHICH HE HIT TRAVELED 400 YDS. IN THE LOW GRAVITY ENVIRONMENT, BOUNDED TWICE, THEN NEST-LED IN THE FINE LUNAR DUST. "NOT BAD FOR A SIX-IRON," SHEPARD COMMENTED!

day of spring, then three years later you'll be planting a month earlier, and after a decade you will be planting in the dead of winter if you don't modify your calendar.

The reason we can't see a "new moon" is that once every 29½ days the moon, so to speak, has its back to us. Since its face is being lit by the sun's rays, its back is merely a darkened shadow!

Who was the first man to map the moon? In the 17th century Johannes Helevius of Danzig charted the moon's surface from a laboratory he constructed on a crowded rooftop in the city. He tried to study more distant objects, but the dust in the atmosphere prevented him from seeing them clearly.

Our moon has no surface phenomena (water, air, volcanic activity) to alter the craters. So they remain unchanged for tens of thousands of years. The only thing likely to alter a crater on the moon is another collision!

The distance between the sun and the Earth is 92,870,000 miles—or 385 times the distance to the moon. Although the sun is so much bigger than the moon it is so much farther away it appears to be about the same size as the moon.

During a total eclipse, the moon fits snugly over the sun, causing temporary near-darkness to occur. The priests of Mesopotamia kept such detailed records of the motions of the heavenly bodies that they could predict lunar eclipses without even understanding what caused them!

WATCHING
THE EARTH
RISE!

You've seen the sun rise and the moon rise, but how about the earth? Well, you can see *our planet* rise, too, *from the moon!* While studying the moon's surface, several satellites have taken pictures of the *rising of the earth!*

ASTRONAUTS NEIL ARMSTRONG
AND JAMES McDIVETT BOTH SAW
UFOs WHILE ON SPACE MISSIONS.
*BUT NASA... ACCORDING TO NEWS-
CASTER WALTER CRONKITE... IS
KEEPING THE EVIDENCE A
SECRET!*

Because the ancient Chinese thought that eclipses were a threat to the Earth, two ancient Chinese court astronomers—Hsi and Ho—were executed for failing to predict an eclipse of the sun. The Chinese believed that eclipses were caused by the appetite of a hungry dragon! To drive the dragon away and bring the sun back, they would run outside and make as much noise as possible.

Fortunately for the Chinese—and us—the moon does not run parallel around us. If it did, we would have eclipses of the sun and moon every time there was a new or a full moon—or in other words, twice every month!

Who took the first photo of the moon? In 1840, John William Draper of England took the first shot. By now, we've been there and, though it's made of materials similar to Earth's, we haven't found any life.

THE AMAZING MOON MACHINES!

The Apollo-11 landing crew brought with them a fabulous collection of *instruments* to measure *almost every aspect* of the moon. They included everything from *seismometers* and a *radio antenna* to a *laser retro-reflector* and a *TV camera!*

The first person to plan a trip to the moon was astronomer Johannes Kepler (1571-1630)—in a science fiction book called *Dream*. In the book the person traveling to the moon uses an anaesthetic —instead of a spacesuit! (Incidentally, Kepler's fantasy described the surface of the moon with uncanny accuracy!)

The strangest object brought back from the moon by the Apollo 12 astronauts is a lemon-shaped rock labeled "12012." It contains 20 times as much uranium, thorium, and potassium as any moon rock previously studied. What's more, it is the oldest moon rock found to date—with an apparent age of 4.6 billion years!

Douglas Aircraft scientist Jack Green has conducted successful experiments where he has actually squeezed water from rocks. Using rocks similar to those on the moon, Green managed to obtain water—by boiling it out of the rocks at a temperature of 300°F. If Green's efforts can be duplicated, astronauts may be able to get their drinking water from the moon's rocks.

The moon, by the way, is the best place we know for an observatory. Since it has almost no atmosphere you could see the sky perfectly—any time of day or night—from two observatories located 180° apart along the moon's equator.

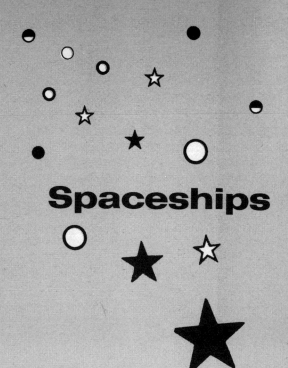

Spaceships

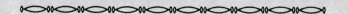

In the 11th century a British monk named Eilmer attached wings to his hands and feet and tried to fly. He made it about an eighth of a mile—then crashed! Eilmer, who was crippled in the mishap, later said he should have added a tail!

The first airship was designed by the Jesuit priest Francesco Lana Tarzi in 1670. Tarzi's drawing was of a canoe with paddles, flown through the air by several glass balloons. Unfortunately, Tarzi's idea never got off the ground, because he felt it would "create many disturbances."

The first successful flight of a balloon was made June 5, 1783 in France. The balloon stayed in the air for a full ten minutes—climbing to a height of 6,000 feet.

Jean-Pierre Blanchard and Dr. John Jeffries were the first people to take an international flight, across the English Channel from Dover to Calais. Blanchard and Jeffries made their flight in a balloon in 1785!

One of the most innovative space scientists ever was Konstantin Tsiolkovsky of Russia. In his science fiction work, *Beyond the Earth,* published in

CANADA

UNITED
STATES

SATELLITE WARS HAVE ALREADY BEGUN!

RUSSIA AND THE U.S. BOTH TRIED TO
SHOOT DOWN AN AILING SOVIET COSMOS
NUCLEAR SATELLITE WITH A SPACE WAR
WEAPON IN JANUARY, 1978. COSMOS
954 WAS OUT OF CONTROL AND FALL-
ING TOWARDS EARTH WITH ITS *100-LB.*
LOAD OF ATOMIC FUEL.

1916, Tsiolkovsky described a space flight almost exactly like the U.S. orbits of the early '60's, including retro rockets for re-entering the Earth! Incidentally, Tsiolkovsky also published a scientific study on the use of liquid-fuel rockets—back in 1898!

The first flight of a liquid-fuel rocket was made on March 16, 1926, by Robert Goddard. The rocket soared to 184 feet in only 2.5 seconds! For three more years Goddard continued his experiments, until the Massachusetts fire marshal put a stop to the rocket tests.

Where did the rocket countdown come from? From a publicity stunt! While serving as technical advisor for the 1928 German space film, "The Girl in the Moon," scientist Hermann Oberth constructed a rocket for it. To add to its launching, he thought of the countdown. Unfortunately, the rocket was never flown—but the countdown has been used ever since.

Five countries have placed artificial satellites in orbit. They are: The United States, the USSR, Japan, France, and the People's Republic of China.

Has space gone to the dogs? The first passenger to travel in a space vehicle was Laika, a Russian dog, who went up in the Soviets' second satellite, Sputnik II, on November 3, 1957.

One satellite, known as Spitz ISTP, can orbit the Earth, fly to the moon, make a loop, and then continue orbiting the moon.

How about a vacation in space? Scientists predict that by 1996 we will have a space colony capable of holding 100,000 people or more. The cost of a one-way trip to the colony, by today's standards, would be about $3,000.

UFO LOOKS AT AIRLINER

On the evening of January 14, 1966, an MIT scientist and three other persons saw an intense white light hovering for about ten minutes over the horizon. The light traveled upwards, stopped, and hovered near a passing airliner!

Every space trip to date has been taken up to a hundred times before the rocket has left Earth. How is that possible? Simple. A computer travels it—to make sure any problems are solved before astronauts can encounter them.

Why is travel in space so difficult? For one thing, there is no strong gravitational pull to tell us which end is up. Also, there's no air to push against in order to be able to steer a spacecraft. And what's worse, space has no absolute speed—which means that in order to get anywhere, a spacecraft has to know the exact speed of its target! Now you know why we can't go out in space without the help of computers!

Food, oxygen and water are the three most vital things every human needs. How much of each do you need each day? Scientists had to answer that question because each astronaut received a package that contained these items. A man needs two pounds of oxygen, 1½ pounds of food, and 4.8 pounds of water per day. Taking into account losses, reserve, and packaging, the weights actually prepared were: 3 pounds of oxygen, 5 pounds of water, and 1.6 pounds of food—or a total of 9.6 pounds per man for each day.

THE FIRST OFFICIAL GOVERN-
MENT PROBE INTO UFOs WAS
ANNOUNCED BY <u>FRANCE</u> IN 1977.
(THE U.S. AGREED TO ASSIST.)

Thinking of building your own space ship? Read this! Building the spacecraft that took astronaut Virgil Grissom into space was a heavy task. This Project Mercury ship had to be able to: go through temperatures from well below zero to 600° above; separate from its "booster" rocket; turn around by itself; slow down in order to come back to Earth; shoot out two parachutes; not fall apart on landing; float without leaking; carry a life raft; be lifted by helicopter; carry a 28-hour supply of oxygen; let the astronaut see outside; keep track of all its functions. Even if the spacecraft managed to do all this, there was still one more problem. It could not weigh more than one ton—or it would never get into space!

Astronaut Virgil Grissom's *Liberty Bell 7* space flight was made with flying colors and near perfection—until he landed in the ocean! While Grissom was inside the capsule waiting to be picked up, the door flew open and water started to pour in. Once outside the capsule, Grissom soon discovered water seeping into his spacesuit. A helicopter picked him up just in time—but the *Liberty Bell 7* capsule went to the bottom of the sea!

On February 20, 1962, John Glenn became the first American in orbit. On his orbit around the Earth, Glenn saw thousands of mysterious particles shortly before sunrise. The bright yellow-green objects quickly disappeared as the sun rose! A NASA scientist later said the particles might have been gas or water molecule clusters from the spacecraft—but he didn't know for sure!

Glenn completed three orbits in his Mercury capsule Friendship 7 in a flight that was far from trouble-free. The automatic control system failed, and Glenn had to fly the Mercury craft himself. And, as Astronaut Glenn was entering his second orbit around the Earth, the "heat shield" on his capsule started to come loose. To try to keep the heat shield in place, part of the spaceship's re-entry rocket was kept on—something that had never been done before! The plan worked—and kept the spaceship from burning up as it re-entered the Earth!

THE FAMED **HOLY SHROUD OF TURIN** IS "NOT A FAKE"... ACCORDING TO NASA SCIENTISTS. SPACE AGE TECHNOLOGY HAS PROVED THAT THE FAMED "PICTURE OF CHRIST" IS ACTUALLY ABOUT **2,000 YEARS OLD**... AND ONCE WAS IN **JERUSALEM**!

HIGHLY SOPHISTICATED COMPUTERS
ARE NOW USED BY <u>GROUND SAUCER
WATCH</u> (GSW) TO CHECK THE AUTH-
ENTICITY OF UFO PICTURES.

According to Soviet astronaut Yuri Gagarin, weightlessness in space is no problem. Said Gagarin during his orbit, "Everything was easier to perform . . . I could have gone on flying through space forever."

What is keeping us from traveling very far out into space? Our rockets—today, they're just not powerful enough to get us much farther than the moon. However, scientists are now experimenting with nuclear rockets. If successful, these could take us at least to Mars!

A spaceship trying to reach our sun's nearest neighbor star would have to travel—at the speed of light—for at least 4½ years! But scientists are already working on ways to get there! One way might be to convert fuel into pure energy so that rockets could travel at the speed of light, 186,000 miles per second. According to Einstein, this is theoretically possible.

Because of gravity, time has no absolute meaning. When you travel very fast, time slows down. Since we are all moving through space, we grow old less quickly than we would if the Earth stood still.

If a spaceship were to travel 580 million miles an hour—or 87% the speed of light—time would be half that of Earth's. A month spent in a spaceship traveling at 677 million miles per hour—or 99.5% the speed of light—would almost equal an entire Earth year. The occupants aboard the spaceship would have no idea anything odd was happening until they returned to Earth. Thus, an expedition to a distant star could leave in 1978 and not return until the next century!

Is space infinite? No scientist knows for sure. But some astronomers say that the Universe has a curved border. Thus, a space explorer will automatically come back to the place from which he started . . . eventually!

Was the film "Star Wars" your first encounter with the laser gun? If so, you're way behind the times! The laser gun was first conceived by H. G. Wells in "The 'War of The Worlds"—the same work that, when broadcast in 1939, sent thousands of people fleeing from their homes because they thought Wells' Martian invasion was real! Wells described his weapon as "a mysterious sword of heat."

Speaking of power sources, UFOs appear to be observing our power plants! Over 100 sightings were reported in a 3-week period in 1977 at the Indian Point Nuclear Power Plant—30 miles from New York City!

Creatures from outer space have already contacted the U.S. Government—according to the Mutual UFO Network. "There is absolutely no doubt," it is reported, "that we are being visited" . . .

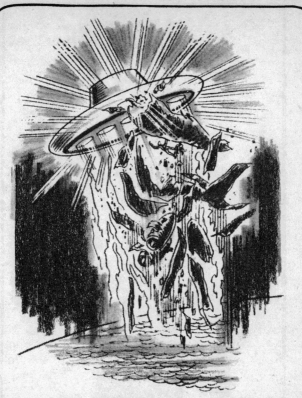

A <u>CLOSE ENCOUNTER</u> BETWEEN AN F-86 BOMBER AND A UFO IN 1957! AN AIR FORCE MAJOR REPORTED SEEING THE BOMBER SMASHING INTO A UFO... THE F-86 DISINTEGRATED AND FELL INTO THE SEA ... BUT THE UFO FLEW BACK INTO THE CLOUDS, APPARENTLY UNDAMAGED!

AIR BASES ARE THREATENED BY <u>LOW-FLYING UFOs</u>! THEY WERE SEEN AT AIR BASES IN MICHIGAN, NORTH DAKOTA, NEW HAMPSHIRE AND CANADA BETWEEN OCT. 28 AND NOV. 12, 1975. THEY FLEW AS LOW AS <u>100 FT.</u> OVER AREAS WHERE NUCLEAR WEAPONS ARE STORED!

ITEM:

August 13, 1956. Approximately 10:00 p.m.: The pilot of a C-47 aircraft flying at about 4,000 feet over Lakenheath, England, and a control tower operator at nearby Bentwaters spotted a "bright light" moving at a "terrific speed" in the sky from east to west. The Bentwaters tower contacted the radar air traffic control center at Lakenheath, which also picked up the UFO on radar. The Royal Air Force then dispatched a Venom fighter to pursue it over Lakenheath. The pilot sighted the UFO and locked it in on his radar fire-control system. However, it disappeared once the plane got within about a half mile of the object.

The radar control center at Lakenheath told the Venom pilot that the UFO had not circled behind him. The fighter was unable to maneuver any closer to it and returned to its base. A second RAF fighter was dispatched, but soon had to return before spotting the UFO because of engine trouble. The Lakenheath radar reported that before leaving its range the object made additional sharp moves, and then traveled north at about 600 miles per hour.

"A UFO HAS CONTACTED ME!" SAYS CAPT. RANDOLPH JENKINS.

"SOME FORM OF TELEPATHY WAS USED TO PROBE *INSIDE MY HEAD.*" THE INCIDENT OCCURRED WHILE HE WAS FLYING HIS JET OVER NEW MEXICO.

ITEM:

November 2, 1957. Approximately 11:00 p.m.: Pedro Saucedo and Joe Salaz were driving a truck just west of Levelland, Texas, when they saw a torpedo-shaped object pass over them. It was moving at between 600 and 800 miles per hour, was about 200 feet long and brightly illuminated. As the object passed over them, the truck's headlights and engine went dead and the two men felt an intense heat. However, after the UFO passed over them, their truck functioned normally.

Following this, Saucedo notified the Levelland police of the incident. About an hour afterward someone else called the police and reported that his automobile engine and headlights had failed as he approached what he described as a 220-foot-long egg-shaped object that was parked on a road. He reported that the object rose up and disappeared when he got out of his car. His car engine could then restart.

During the night, the Levelland police received several other reports of UFO sightings. They all generally matched the first two reports in describing the size and shape of the object and the malfunctioning automobiles. While investigating, a sheriff and his deputy observed an oval-shaped light crossing the highway a few hundred yards ahead of them, while two patrolmen following them saw a similar flash in the direction of their car.

In total, seven cases of sightings with automobile malfunctions and three without any
physical effects were reported to the police
of that small Texas town that night. Strangely,
several other UFO incidents were reported
that night and the next in the same general
area of Texas and nearby New Mexico. In
dozens of reported sightings, people indicated that their cars stopped functioning—
when a UFO was nearby!

ITEM:

January, 1963. Eyewitnesses reported an
egg-shaped object descending toward Earth
in Tucuman, Argentina. Local scientists later
studied the scorched rings found there and
stated that the grass roots within these rings
appeared to have been scorched and dried
up without combustion by a temperature of
more than 2,000°C. About 10 years later, on
September 10th, 1973, an egg-shaped object
was seen over Griffin, Ga. Shortly thereafter
a depression was noted in the soil, which
recorded a temperature of 200 to 300°F!

BRIAN SCOTT OF GARDEN GROVE,
CALIFORNIA, HAS BEEN ABDUCTED
FOUR TIMES BY WEIRD AND FRIGHT-
ENING BEINGS SINCE HIS FIRST
ENCOUNTER IN 1971.'

"THE THING IS CLIMBING" WITH THESE FOUR WORDS, AIR FORCE PILOT TOM MANTELL SET OFF IN PURSUIT OF A <u>*RED AND WHITE METALLIC UFO*</u> ON JANUARY 7, 1948. THE WRECKAGE OF MANTELL'S PLANE WAS LATER DISCOVERED STREWN OVER THE ENTIRE VICINITY. NO ONE KNOWS WHAT CAUSED THE CRASH.

ITEM:

Socorro, New Mexico. 6:00 p.m. on April 24, 1964: Local police officer Lonnie Zamora was chasing a speeder when something interrupted him. He heard a roar and then saw a bluish-white flame descending about ¾ of a mile away. Suddenly the sound stopped and Zamora did not see the object again until he drove up a steep hill. There on the ground, about 200 yards to the south, he saw a shiny, aluminum-like object, egg-shaped, with two legs supporting it. Next to it were two figures in white coveralls. They appeared below average in height, "normal in shape," and one seemed to be startled at the officer's presence.

As Zamora left his car and approached the object he heard a banging sound and saw that the coveralled figures had vanished. With another roar the UFO slowly lifted off the ground, a flame under it. Zamora also noticed a large red insignia on the craft. The UFO headed south-east and moved rapidly in a straight line, but only about 10 to 15 feet off the ground. It disappeared after it cleared a nearby mountain, traveling in the air without flames, smoke or noise.

State police, FBI and Air Force personnel later joined Zamora in returning to the site, and they saw bent and burned brush in several places. Some of the witnesses measured the distance between four indentations in the sand; it was between a half inch to two inches deep. These four indentations formed a quadrilateral whose diagonals intersected at right angles. The mid-point of its sides defined a circle whose center coincided with the chief fire scar left by the object.

ITEM:

On the evening of November 2, 1967 two Navajo Indians, Willie Begay and Guy Tossie, were driving on Highway 26 near Ririe, Idaho, when a bright flash of light and a small UFO appeared directly in front of their car. They said that it was shaped like two saucers placed rim to rim, was about five to eight feet in diameter, about two feet thick, and

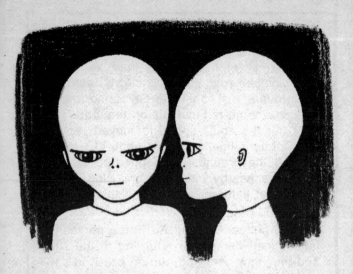

2 MEN... AIR FORCE
SGT. CHARLES L. MOODY
AND TRAVIS WALTON...
BOTH CLAIMED TO HAVE MET
CREATURES FROM
OUTER SPACE!
THEY DREW AMAZINGLY SIMILAR
PICTURES - OF THE VERY SAME
CREATURE ... <u>YET THEY NEVER
MET EACH OTHER</u>!

had a transparent dome on its top. Two occupants could be seen inside.

As the two men's car was brought to a stop, different colored lights began flashing through holes around the outside of the object. Soon, a 3½-foot creature appeared from the opened dome, floated toward the car, opened the door and entered it. Wearing coveralls and a high backpack, it had—according to the Indians—rough, scarred skin, high ears, round eyes, a slit for a mouth and was without a nose.

Begay and Tossie's car was towed to a field, whereupon Begay jumped out and ran to a nearby farmhouse, with one of the UFO occupants in pursuit. The other one remained in the car and talked to Tossie in an unintelligible voice. The first creature soon returned and the two re-entered the UFO. It rose in a zig-zag pattern, with a yellow light flaming from the bottom of the vehicle. Turning very bright, it rapidly disappeared.

After several minutes, Begay returned with Willard Hammon, a farmer. He accompanied the two Navajos to the police to report the incident. Although the two men admitted that they had been drinking beer, investigators and witnesses agreed that they were not drunk.

At about 11:30 that same evening, on another highway near Ririe, a truck was stopped by a small UFO descending in front of it. A small man got out of the vehicle and tried to enter the truck. The driver told a UFO investigator that he managed to evade the creature and drive away.

ITEM:

January, 1975. North Bergen, N.J.: Liquor store owner George O'Barski was driving through North Hudson Park in North Bergen at about 3:00 a.m. when he began to notice some interference on his car radio. Soon the signal faded and O'Barski heard a droning hum to his left. Then a bright object flew past, stopped, and hovered a few feet over a park lawn. The object was a circular vehicle, about 30 feet across, flat on the bottom, with vertical sides and a convex roof that was about 8 feet from the bottom. The craft had about a dozen oblong, vertical windows that were spaced equally around it and a light shining through its windows that illuminated the area.

O'Barski reported that a ladder descended from the UFO, a door opened, and eight to eleven 3½' tall creatures came out. They were dressed in helmets and jump-suits, and appeared to scoop up samples of soil and put them in bags. They then returned to their vehicle, which ascended rapidly and disappeared. O'Barski returned to the park the next day and found a series of holes in the ground 4" to 5" wide and 6" deep. Several other UFO sightings were reported in the same area that month with two of them closely corresponding to O'Barski's testimony. Evidence indicates that these two sightings occurred on the same night as O'Barski's.

CORP. ARMANDO VALDES LOST 5 DAYS OF HIS LIFE... <u>IN 15 MINUTES</u>! WITNESSES CONFIRM THAT HE WAS SEIZED BY A UFO AND HELD FOR 15 MINUTES. BUT WHEN HE REAPP- EARED HIS CALENDAR WATCH HAD ADVANCED BY 5 DAYS AND <u>HE HAD A SUDDEN, 5-DAY GROWTH OF BEARD ON HIS FACE</u>!

In 1965, the government of Argentina issued the first official communiqué documenting the sighting of a UFO. According to the report, Argentinian, Chilean, and British sailors stationed at Deception Island naval bases in Antarctica spotted a red, green, and yellow flying object that made no sound, zig-zagged across the sky, and also hovered at a height of 15,000 feet for about 20 minutes. In conclusion, the official government document noted, "The occurrence was witnessed by scientists of the three naval bases and . . . the facts by those people agree completely."

ITEM:

July 4, 1975. Parsippany, N.J.: A college student and his date were returning from the movies when they spotted a cigar-shaped object about 60 to 80 feet long, moving slowly parallel to the ground and only 75 feet or so in the air. They heard no sound, but observed a bright light coming from the vehicle, illuminating the surrounding area, yet with no glare. The witnesses also noticed a pattern of blue-green, white, and red lights coming from different parts of the object. The white light was coming from the front bottom and appeared to sweep the ground for a moment. The object then moved about and hovered for a few minutes before whizzing off into the sky in a flash.

At about 10:00 p.m. that same evening, pilot Jim Quodomine and his fiancée met another couple at Caldwell Airfield near Parsippany. They pointed out to Quodomine a UFO in the distance quite similar to the one seen in the early morning by the college student. The object was clearly visible as a large white light, so Quodomine and his fiancée took off in pursuit of it in his private plane. They came within four or five miles of the object at an altitude of 3,000 feet. They confirmed the other witnesses' description. When Quodomine tried to approach the UFO at about 100 miles per hour it changed brightness, moved away rapidly and disappeared in seconds!

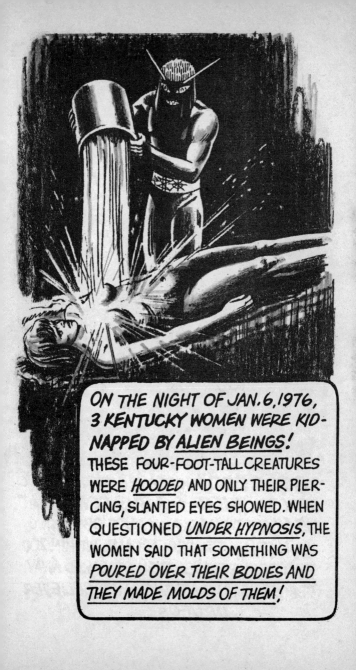

ON THE NIGHT OF JAN. 6, 1976, 3 KENTUCKY WOMEN WERE KIDNAPPED BY _ALIEN BEINGS_! THESE FOUR-FOOT-TALL CREATURES WERE _HOODED_ AND ONLY THEIR PIERCING, SLANTED EYES SHOWED. WHEN QUESTIONED _UNDER HYPNOSIS_, THE WOMEN SAID THAT SOMETHING WAS _POURED OVER THEIR BODIES AND THEY MADE MOLDS OF THEM_!

"GOOD GOD," SCREAMED CAPT. FRANCO DEROSA, "THERE'S A BUS COMING AT US!" BUT IT WAS REALLY A UFO OBSERVING HIS ALITALIA JETLINER. IT CAME WITHIN 200 FEET OF THE PLANE...THEN STREAKED AWAY. DEROSA IS NOW A CONFIRMED BELIEVER IN UFOs!

ITEM:

August, 1897: Two young children with green skin and slanted eyes were discovered in a cave in the Catalonian region of Spain. They wore clothing made of an unknown fabric and spoke a curious language that professors from the University of Barcelona were unable to identify.

The boy died, but the girl eventually learned to speak Spanish. She said that she came from a place where it is "always twilight." She and her brother had been transported to that remote cave by a mysterious "whirlwind." No explanation has ever been found for this, one of the strangest cases on record!

Believe It or Not!

Glossary

ANGSTROM — a small distance, 10^{-10} of a meter.

ANNULAR ECLIPSE — a solar eclipse where the sun's surface peeks around the moon's edge and produces a circle of light.

ANTIELECTRON — *see* positron.

ANTIMATTER — the opposite of matter. Matter and antimatter may, on collision, cancel each other, leaving only energy.

ASTEROIDS — small solid bodies whose orbits around the sun are usually between Mars and Jupiter.

ASTRONOMICAL UNIT — the distance between the earth and sun: 93 million miles.

ATOM — a tiny object that has a nucleus and one or more orbiting electrons. The number of protons in the nucleus determines which element the atom represents.

AURORA — glowing night-time lights. Produced by the interaction of the solar wind with the earth's magnetic field and atmosphere.

AXIS — an imaginary line from the north pole through the center of the earth to the south pole.

BIG-BANG COSMOLOGY — a theory of the origin of the universe in which the entire universe originated in one explosive Big Bang.

BINARY STARS — two stars in orbit about each other.

BLACK HOLE — an object whose gravity is so high that nothing can escape, not even light.

BLUE GIANT — a large, hot star.

CHROMOSPHERE — the layer of the sun's atmosphere just about the photosphere.

CLUSTER OF GALAXIES — a clumping of galaxies.

COMET — a small, icy, dusty object that, as it approaches the sun, becomes visible as a glowing ball with a long tail.

CONCAVE MIRROR — a mirror that is curved inward.

CONSTELLATION — any group of stars in the sky which appear to form a pattern.

CONVEX MIRROR — a mirror that is curved outward.

CORE (EARTH'S) — the hot nickel-iron region of the earth.

COSMIC RAYS — high energy atomic particles that strike the earth's atmosphere.

COSMOLOGY — the study of the universe as a whole.

CRESCENT MOON — a phase of the moon from which you can see less than half the moon.

CRUST (EARTH'S) — the outer layer of the earth.

DAY — the time it takes for the earth to rotate once.

DIFFRACTION — the bending of light.

DISH (RADIO) — the large surface of a radio telescope that reflects radio waves.

DNA (DEOXYRIBONUCLEIC ACID) — the long-chained molecule which contains the genetic code and can reproduce itself.

DUST CLOUDS — clouds of small particles in space that absorb light.

DWARF STAR — a star of less-than-average diameter.

DWARF GALAXY — a smaller-than-average galaxy.

ECLIPSE — the total or partial obscurtaion of one celestial body by another.

ELECTRON — a negatively charged particle that is found in orbit around the nucleus of an atom.

ELEMENT — a type of atom, classification of which is based on the number of protons in the nucleus.

FIREBALL — meteor that is bright enough to be visible in the daytime.

FIRST-QUARTER MOON — a phase of the moon in which one half is illuminated.

FULL MOON — the phase of the moon in which you see the moon's entire hemisphere.

GALAXY — a collection of stars held together by mutual gravitation.

GIANT PLANETS — Jupiter, Saturn, Uranus, and Neptune.

GIBBOUS MOON — a phase of the moon between first and third quarters.

GRAVITY — the attraction of one mass to another.

HALLEY'S COMET — comet named after Edmond Halley (1656-1742) who studied records of comets back to 1531 and who predicted that this one would return in 1758. It appeared on Christmas night of that year. 1986 is the scheduled year of its next reappearance.

HYDROGEN BURNING — the fusion of hydrogen to produce helium.

LIGHT-WEEK — the distance light travels in one week (1.5×10^{11} miles).

LIGHT-YEAR — the distance light travels in one year (6×10^{12} miles).

LUNAR ECLIPSE — an eclipse of the moon by earth.

METEOR — the luminous streak of light caused by the rapid entry and atmospheric frictional heating of a piece of interplanetary material. Also termed "shooting star."

METEOR SHOWER — meteors that seem to fall out of a certain point in the sky simultaneously.

METEORITE — a meteor particle that has fallen to the earth's surface.

MILKY WAY — our own galaxy.

MOLECULE — two or more atoms that are bound together.

MOON — the earth's only known natural satellite. It shines from the sun's reflected light.

NEBULA — any diffuse astronomical object.

NEUTRON — a neutral particle that is about 2,000 times more massive than an electron.

NOVA — the sudden brightening of a star.

NEUTRON — an electrically neutral particle in the nucleus of an atom. It has the same mass as a proton.

OPTICAL TELESCOPE — a telescope designed to produce an image using visible light.

ORBIT — the path which an object follows when revolving around another.

PERIODIC TABLE — an organized listing of all the elements.

PLANET — one of the bodies, except a comet, meteor or satellite, that revolves around the sun in the solar system.

PLANETARY NEBULA — a shell of glowing gas surrounding a hot central star.

POSITRON — similar to an electron and having the same mass but positively charged.

PRISM — a wedged-shape glass that disperses light to produce a spectrum.

PROTON — a charged particle found in the nucleus of an atom.

PULSAR — a rapidly rotating neutron star that emits radio waves in pulses.

PULSATING STAR — a star that expands and contracts, and alters its light intensity.

QUASARS — objects of stellar appearance with energy output generally exceeding that of galaxies.

RADIO ASTRONOMY — the field of astronomy concerned with the observation of radio waves of astronomical origin.

RAINBOW — an arc or circle that exhibits in concentric bands the colors of the spectrum and that is formed opposite the sun by the refraction and reflection of the sun's rays in raindrops, spray, or mist.

RED GIANT — a large, luminous star with a cool surface.

REFRACTING TELESCOPE — a telescope whose objective is a lens.

SATELLITE — an object that is in orbit around another object.

SHOCK WAVE — a very strong sound-wave impulse.

SHOOTING STAR — *see* meteor.

SOLAR ECLIPSE — an eclipse of the sun by the moon.

SOLAR SYSTEM — the sun's family. This includes all objects around the sun: planets, satellites, asteroids, and comets.

SOLAR WIND — the outward flow of particles (electrons, protons, etc.) from the sun.

SPECTRUM — the array of colors or intensities of radiation at different wavelengths presented in order of their wavelengths.

STAR — a gaseous sphere held together by its own gravity, one massive enough to provide internal temperatures needed for nuclear burning.

STELLAR PARALLAX — the shift in apparent position of a star, as observed from the earth on opposite sides of its orbit.

STRATOSPHERE — a layer in the earth's atmosphere starting about 10 kilometers (6 miles) above the surface.

SUN — a medium-sized, middle-aged star, 4.6 billion years old; center of our solar system.

SUNSPOT — a dark, relatively cool spot on the surface of the sun; typically 1000 kilometers in diameter; associated with strong magnetic fields.

SUPERNOVA — a star that explodes with a hundred-billion fold increase in luminosity.

TERRESTRIAL PLANETS — Mercury, Venus, Earth, and Mars; the planets composed mainly of rock iron, resembling the earth.

TOTAL ECLIPSE — an eclipse of the moon for which the moon is entirely within the shadow of the earth.

TRIPLE STAR — three stars that remain in orbit about each other.

UMBRA — the darkest, central portion of a sunspot.

UNIVERSE — the totality of matter, energy, and space.

WAVELENGTH — the distance between two successive crests or valleys in a wave.

WHITE DWARF — a small hot star that is near or at the end of its nuclear burning.

YEAR — the time it takes for the earth to revolve once around the sun.